# Inventory of Mammals at Walnut Canyon, Wupatki, and Sunset Crater National Monuments

Natural Resource Technical Report NPS/SCPN/NRTR—2009/278

## Author

Charles Drost
U.S. Geological Survey Southwest Biological Science Center
2255 N. Gemini Drive
Flagstaff, AZ 86001

## Editing and Design

Jean Palumbo
National Park Service, Southern Colorado Plateau Network
Northern Arizona University
Flagstaff, Arizona

December 2009

U.S. Department of the Interior
National Park Service
Natural Resource Program Center
Fort Collins, Colorado

The National Park Service, Natural Resource Program Center publishes a range of reports that address natural resource topics of interest and applicability to a broad audience in the National Park Service and others in natural resource management, including scientists, conservation and environmental constituencies, and the public.

The Natural Resource Technical Report Series is used to disseminate results of scientific studies in the physical, biological, and social sciences for both the advancement of science and the achievement of the National Park Service mission. The series provides contributors with a forum for displaying comprehensive data that are often deleted from journals because of page limitations.

All manuscripts in the series receive the appropriate level of peer review to ensure that the information is scientifically credible, technically accurate, appropriately written for the intended audience, and designed and published in a professional manner. This report received formal peer review by subject-matter experts who were not directly involved in the collection, analysis, or reporting of the data, and whose background and expertise put them on par technically and scientifically with the authors of the information.

Views, statements, findings, conclusions, recommendations, and data in this report are those of the author(s) and do not necessarily reflect views and policies of the National Park Service, U.S. Department of the Interior. Mention of trade names or commercial products does not constitute endorsement or recommendation for use by the National Park Service.

This project was funded through the Colorado Plateau Cooperative Ecosystem Studies Unit, Northern Arizona University, under Cooperative Agreement H1200040002, task agreements NAU-64 and NAU-101.

This report is available electronically from the Southern Colorado Plateau Network website (http://www.nature.nps.gov/im/units/SCPN) and the Natural Resource Publications Management Web site (http://www.nature.nps.gov/publications/NRPM) on the Internet.

Please cite this publication as:

Drost, C. 2009. Inventory of mammals at Walnut Canyon, Wupatki, and Sunset Crater National Monuments. Natural Resource Technical Report NPS/SCPN/NRTR—2009/278. National Park Service, Fort Collins, Colorado.

NPS 360/100791, December 2009

# Contents

# Figures

# Tables

# Abstract

This report documents the results of a mammal inventory study of Walnut Canyon National Monument (WACA) and Wupatki National Monument (WUPA) in north-central Arizona near the city of Flagstaff. We also include results of bat surveys and reviews of literature and museum specimen data for Sunset Crater Volcano National Monument, also in the Flagstaff area. Fieldwork for the inventory focused on small mammals, primarily bats and rodents. Methods used in field surveys for bats included acoustic surveys using Anabat, along with mist-netting at stock tanks and other water bodies. Most of the bat survey work was conducted in 2000, with additional fieldwork in 2002 and 2003. Fieldwork for terrestrial small mammals used trapping with Sherman and Tomahawk small- and medium-sized mammal traps, along with visual surveys for diurnal species. The majority of field sampling for terrestrial small mammals was carried out from 2002 through 2004. In addition to field sampling, we reviewed, evaluated, and summarized museum and literature records of mammal species for the three monuments.

A total of 48 native mammal species are currently known to occur at WACA. Two additional species (bighorn sheep and coati) were present historically but no longer occur in the area, and at least one non-native species (domestic cattle) occurs as occasional trespass animals. At WUPA, there are also 48 documented native mammal species, and three additional non-native species. Of these totals, 16 species are new for WACA (positively documented for the first time), and seven are new for WUPA. Noteworthy additions at WACA include Allen's big-eared bat, big free-tailed bat, and white-backed hog-nosed skunk. Significant new species at WUPA include spotted bat, big free-tailed bat, and kit fox.

# Acknowledgments

Funding for this work was provided by the National Park Service as part of their Inventory and Monitoring program. The USGS Southwest Biological Science Center contributed the funding and time for the project leader / report author. This project owes much to the field staff who carried out most of the sampling and data collection at Walnut Canyon and Wupatki National Monuments. Their hard work, care, and diligence in field work and data handling provided the foundation for this report. Thanks go to Lisa Gelczis, Mary Ellen Prince, and Jenohn Wrieden (2002), Amanda Matthews and Kristen Pearson (2003), and Garrett Holway, and Wendy and David Tidhar (2004). The excellent results of the bat sampling are primarily due to Chris Corben and his great knowledge and expertise with Anabat. Thanks also to National Park Service staff for their assistance and advice on accessing different areas of the two monuments, and for sharing their knowledge of the monuments. Special thanks are due Mary Blasing (Wupatki National Monument), and John Portillo (Walnut Canyon National Monument). Review of local museum holdings added greatly to this project. For assistance with access to their holdings, we thank Janet Gillette at the Museum of Northern Arizona, and Tad Theimer, curator of the mammal collection at Northern Arizona University. Finally, I thank the staff of the Southern Colorado Plateau Network of the NPS – especially Anne Cully and Nicole Tancreto – for their help with administration, oversight, and aspects of the coordination of this project.

# 1 Introduction

One of the major purposes of the U. S. National Park Service (NPS) is to protect and preserve the plants, animals, and biological communities of the federal lands that it manages. This is stated in the agency's founding legislation, which describes the mission of the Park Service as "…to conserve the scenery and the natural and historic objects and the wild life therein…" of the lands that they manage (National Park Service Organic Act, 1916). As a fundamental part of this mission, NPS policy explicitly recognizes the important need for basic inventory data of natural resources. NPS management policies state: "The National Park Service will assemble baseline inventory data describing the natural resources under its stewardship and will monitor those resources at regular intervals to detect or predict changes" (NPS Management Policies 4:4 1988). For a nationwide network of parks, monuments, historic sites, recreation areas, and other lands, however, putting policy into practice can be a challenge. Even large, well-known areas such as Grand Canyon National Park are deficient in aspects of basic inventory data, and many small NPS areas have received very little study (Stohlgren and Quinn 1992).

The National Park Service renewed its focus on natural resource inventory and monitoring in 1992 with the creation of an agency-wide Inventory and Monitoring Program. In fiscal year 2000, NPS initiated a national program to inventory vertebrates and vascular plants within all park areas that have significant natural resources. As part of this effort, all NPS lands were divided into 32 groups or "networks," based on geographical proximity and similar habitat types. The many NPS areas on the Colorado Plateau of eastern Utah, northern Arizona, northwestern New Mexico, and western Colorado were divided into the Northern Colorado Plateau Network and the Southern Colorado Plateau Network. Within each network, working groups of NPS managers, natural resources specialists, and outside cooperators developed inventory plans. These plans included reviews of existing knowledge, an evaluation and prioritization of inventory needs for vertebrates and vascular plants, and methodologies for conducting, evaluating, and reporting inventory work.

Walnut Canyon National Monument (WACA) and Wupatki National Monument (WUPA) with estimated inventory completeness of 70% and 85 %, respectively, were both designated as "first priority" for inventory studies of mammals within the Southern Colorado Plateau Network (SCPN; Stuart 2000),. The network plan identified both areas as being in need of "basic inventory" work, i.e. surveys to determine overall species composition, as well as to provide general information on distribution and relative abundance. Small mammals (rodents, bats, etc.) were identified as a specific priority for both areas. During our review of species lists, literature, and museum records for this project, it became apparent that a well-documented, comprehensive list had never been prepared for Sunset Crater National Monument either, so we have added an annotated list for SUCR to this report, based on limited recent fieldwork, and a thorough review of literature and museum specimens.

This report

1. describes the specific methods and results of inventory work on mammal species at WACA and WUPA,

2. evaluates the current state of inventory completeness

3. discusses the mammal communities of the two monuments, with particular emphasis on protection and management.

In line with the overall goals described in the Southern Colorado Plateau Network inventory plan (Stuart 2000), the objectives of the project described here were to: (1) develop up-to-date mammal species lists for WACA, WUPA, and SUCR; (2) summarize population data, such as distribution and relative abundance of the mammal species at WACA and WUPA; (3) provide data from the inventory work, both in tabular and spatial form; and (4) outline considerations for NPS management, monitoring, and additional research needs. We also provide summaries of biological and natural history information yielded by the survey work. We also provide summaries of biological and natural history information yielded by the survey work.

# 2 Study Areas

## 2.1 Walnut Canyon National Monument

WACA is located in north-central Arizona, about 13 km (8 miles) east-southeast of the city of Flagstaff. Elevation ranges from approximately 2,091 m (6,861 ft) along the south rim of Walnut Canyon near the southwest corner of the monument, to 1,896 m (6,221 ft.) on the canyon bottom at the northeast / downstream end of the monument. The monument was initially established in 1915, and its boundaries were expanded in 1938 and again in 1996 to its current area of 1,433 ha (ca. 3,540 acres; NPS 2003, 2007). The monument was established to protect cliff dwellings and associated archaeological resources of the Northern Sinagua culture. In addition to the archaeological sites that it preserves, park management documents also note the diversity of biological resources within WACA, with ecological communities ranging from ponderosa pine and Douglas fir forest on the canyon rims and slopes, to pinyon-juniper woodland and savanna, to riparian woodland on the canyon bottom (NPS 2007). A small area of grassland is located in the eastern end of the most recent addition to the monument's extent. This wide range of vegetation communities provides habitat for an equally diverse range of animal species.

Currently, visitation to WACA is confined to the north rim area of the canyon. Visitor access is limited to the "Island Trail," "Rim Trail," and occasional ranger-led hikes to sites west of the visitor center and Ranger Cabin. Management issues at Walnut Canyon include (1) encroaching development from the city of Flagstaff, (2) increased visitation and associated impacts on cultural and natural resources, (3) effects of fire exclusion and the threat of catastrophic wildfire, (4) restoration of species and habitats, particularly the canyon-bottom riparian area, (5) alteration of seasonal water flow in the canyon, and (6) protection of rare wildlife and plant species (NPS 2007).

Most previous inventory work at WACA has focused on the flora of the area, with little work on animal species. Salomonson (1973) reviewed existing museum and sightings records and conducted limited fieldwork to produce a review of mammal species known from the monument. Many of the species on this list were noted as "hypothetical"— they were not positively known from within the monument, but were thought to be probably present, based on their occurrence in surrounding areas. The list portion of this report was reprinted as a park checklist (Salomonson 1985). Unfortunately, reference to "hypothetical" occurrence was removed from this list, giving the impression of greater certainty in the list than was originally intended. This has caused confusion about the known status of mammals at WACA. Overall, many aspects of the mammal fauna of the monument remain poorly known.

## 2.2 Wupatki National Monument

WUPA is located approximately 42 km (26 miles) north-northeast of Flagstaff, in north-central Arizona. Elevation at WUPA ranges from approximately 1,749 m (5,738 ft.) on the broad slope at the southwest corner of the monument, to approximately 1,304 m (4,278 ft.) along the Little Colorado River at the northeast corner of the monument. WUPA was established as a national monument in 1924 to protect ruins and associated archaeological resources representing prehistoric Puebloan cultures in this area. The monument's enabling legislation specifically notes the significance of the WUPA archaeological sites to contemporary native tribes in northern Arizona. When it was first established, WUPA comprised two separate small areas protecting the Wupatki Pueblo and the Citadel site. Boundary expansion in 1937, and subsequent boundary adjustments in 1941, 1961, and 1996 enlarged the monument to its current area of 14,291 ha (ca. 35,422 acres; NPS 2002a). From the standpoint of natural resources, WUPA protects unusual earth-crack caves, as well as a significant area of native grassland that has been protected from domestic grazing since 1989. Habitats at the monument are divided into desert scrub vegetation east of the Doney Cliffs, juniper savanna and grassland on the uplands west of the Doney Cliffs, and a limited amount of riparian habitat along the Little Colorado River on the east border of the monument.

Most visitation to the monument is concentrated at the sites of individual ruins that are open to the public, and the trails associated with those sites. There are occasional ranger-guided backcountry hikes, and some amount of unauthorized off-road and off-trail use occurs. Management concerns include (1) non-native species, (2) effects of water withdrawals, (3) effects of past cattle grazing and fire exclusion, and (4) Native American uses (NPS 2002a).

## 2.3 Sunset Crater Volcano National Monument

We conducted limited work at Sunset Crater National Monument (SUCR)—primarily bat surveys and a review of museum specimens. SUCR encompasses 1,230 ha (3,040 acres) and is located approximately 21 km (13 miles) north-northeast of Flagstaff in north-central Arizona. Elevation at SUCR ranges from 2,450 m (8,039 ft., recorded on benchmark) on the rim of Sunset Crater itself, down to approximately 2,081 m (6,829 ft) at the bottom of a natural sink at the southwest base of Sunset Crater. This area was established as a national monument on May 26, 1930 to protect Sunset Crater and the surrounding volcanic formations (NPS, 2002b). The general management plan for the site describes the monument's purpose as "to preserve and protect Sunset Crater Volcano National Monument's geological formations, features, and resources for scientific interests and research, and for public interest, including scenic, educational, and recreational pursuits" (NPS 2002b). Land cover types at SUCR include extensive areas of sparsely vegetated cinders and lava flows. The most extensive well-vegetated areas are open ponderosa pine / apache plume woodlands, with much more limited areas of grassland and pinyon-juniper communities (Hansen et al. 2004).

Staff and students from Northern Arizona University conducted a series of biological surveys and studies of SUCR and WUPA, which are described in a series of reports containing several chapters on mammals (Bateman 1976, 1980, 1981). Mammal surveys by Bateman's group primarily focused on trapping for small mammals, and were limited in intensity and geographic coverage. An earlier thesis study (Lincoln

1961) compared past and present mammal faunas in this region. Both Bateman and Lincoln listed combined data for the area of SUCR and WUPA, with no separate listing of species, abundance or ecological data for each of the two monuments. The practice of lumping information from SUCR and WUPA was also followed on National Park Service "Observation Record" cards, on file at the Flagstaff Area National Monuments office. It cannot be clearly determined if the information on many of these cards refers to SUCR, WUPA, or both. Lincoln (1961) also provided an overall mammal species list for the broad geographic region of the Wupatki / San Francisco Mountains area.

All of this has led to some confusion as to what mammal species have been documented within the boundaries of WUPA, and what species have been documented at SUCR. A good example is Abert's squirrel (*Sciurus aberti*), which has been included on mammal checklists for WUPA, presumably based on cards labeled "Wupatki." Observation card records for Abert's squirrel are clearly based on information from SUCR. No reliable records exist for this tree squirrel from within or near Wupatki, and habitat at the monument is unsuitable for this species, which is closely tied to ponderosa pine forest. Nonetheless, the studies noted above (and particularly museum records) do provide useful comparative information when the data for particular species are sorted out. Hoffmeister (1986) also includes specimen records for SUCR and WUPA, but these are scattered throughout the general species accounts in his book on the mammals of Arizona.

Several known sensitive mammal species occur in the area of WUPA, including the Wupatki pocket mouse (*Perognathus amplus cineris*), spotted bat (*Euderma maculatum*), and Townsend's big-eared bat (*Corynorhinus townsendii*).

# 3 Methods

## 3.1 Sampling Design

Following the guidance of the SCPN plan (Stuart 2000), field sampling was focused on small mammals, primarily rodents and

**Table 1.** Random sampling points at Walnut Canyon National Monument. Points are stratified by four major habitats at Walnut Canyon (see text). UTM datum is NAD 27.

| Site number | UTM | Habitat |
| --- | --- | --- |
| WACA-174 | 451096 / 3891453 | Ponderosa Pine |
| WACA-505 | 452347 / 3891922 | Ponderosa Pine |
| WACA-628 | 452816 / 3891922 | Ponderosa Pine |
| WACA-735 | 453129 / 3895831 | Ponderosa Pine |
| WACA-1071 | 454536 / 3890671 | Ponderosa Pine |
| WACA-1194 | 455005 / 3890671 | Ponderosa Pine |
| WACA-955 | 454067 / 3891766 | Juniper Woodland |
| WACA-1010 | 454223 / 3893955 | Juniper Woodland |
| WACA-1047 | 454380 / 3893329 | Juniper Woodland |
| WACA-1476 | 456100 / 3889890 | Juniper Woodland |
| WACA-1603 | 456569 / 3890515 | Juniper Woodland |
| WACA-1732 | 457038 / 3891453 | Juniper Woodland |
| WACA-2393 | 459520 / 3892287 | Grassland |
| WACA-752 | 453285 / 3892079 | Canyon bottom |
| WACA-2190 | 458758 / 3892548 | Canyon bottom |
| WACA-2273 | 459070 / 3892704 | Canyon bottom |

bats. Sampling sites were divided between (1) points selected as a stratified-random sample of both monuments and (2) points selected to target specific habitats or particular species of interest. The number of random points for both monuments was calculated based on the number of samples required to achieve 90% inventory completeness (i.e. 90% of the estimated number of species at each monument). This calculation used the number of species that we had estimated to be in each area (S) and the number of species we expected to detect, on average, in a single plot (MS). Details on the calculations and the resulting numbers are provided in Stuart (2000). Both areas were divided into grid cells and a subset of the cells was selected for each area. In the field, we set traps in a transect at the grid center. The calculations resulted in the selection of 16 random points for WACA and 33 for WUPA (Tables 1 and 2). Random points at WACA were stratified into four vegetation types (in order of the number of points and extent of the habitat): Ponderosa Pine Woodland (6); Juniper Woodland (6); Canyon Bottom/Riparian (3); and Grassland (1). Points at WUPA were stratified into four vegetation types: Grassland (10); Shadscale Scrub (10); Juniper Woodland (7); and Desert Wash (6).

We used additional targeted (or "purposive") sampling to survey microhabitats of particular interest and to verify the presence of unconfirmed species from our hypothetical species lists for each monument (see Appendices 1 and 2). Targeted sampling was based on the investigators' knowledge of species habitat requirements and field evaluation of habitats within the survey area. Targeted species included both nocturnal small mammals, sampled primarily by live-trapping methods; and diurnal mammals, detected primarily by visual surveys during daylight hours. Some of the nocturnal small mammals that we specifically targeted included Mogollon vole (*Microtus mogollonensis*), northern grasshopper mouse (*Onychomys leucogaster*), and western harvest mouse (*Reithrodontomys megalotis*), all at WACA. Diurnal target species included cliff chipmunk (*Neotamias dorsalis*) at both monuments, and spotted ground squirrel (*Spermophilus spilosoma*) at WUPA.

We selected the most efficient sampling methods to specifically survey small- and medium-sized mammal species known or expected to occur at WACA and WUPA (Jones et al. 1996). The methods used also

**Table 2.** Random sampling points at Wupatki National Monument. Points are stratified by four major habitats at Wupatki (see text). UTM datum is NAD 27.

| Site number | UTM | Habitat |
| --- | --- | --- |
| WUPA-417 | 453199 / 3934979 | Juniper Woodland |
| WUPA-693 | 454587 / 3933869 | Juniper Woodland |
| WUPA-977 | 455976 / 3934979 | Juniper Woodland |
| WUPA-1256 | 457364 / 3934702 | Juniper Woodland |
| WUPA-1309 | 457642 / 3933869 | Juniper Woodland |
| WUPA-1371 | 457920 / 3935535 | Juniper Woodland |
| WUPA-1642 | 459308 / 3933036 | Juniper Woodland |
| WUPA-2372 | 462918 / 3933591 | Desert Wash |
| WUPA-2427 | 463196 / 3933313 | Desert Wash |
| WUPA-2433 | 463196 / 3934979 | Desert Wash |
| WUPA-2546 | 463751 / 3935257 | Desert Wash |
| WUPA-2602 | 464029 / 3935257 | Desert Wash |
| WUPA-2717 | 464584 / 3936090 | Desert Wash |
| WUPA-3160 | 466806 / 3934702 | Shadscale Scrub |
| WUPA-3280 | 467361 / 3936923 | Shadscale Scrub |
| WUPA-3312 | 467639 / 3930259 | Shadscale Scrub |
| WUPA-3330 | 467639 / 3935257 | Shadscale Scrub |
| WUPA-3584 | 469027 / 3928037 | Shadscale Scrub |
| WUPA-3827 | 470138 / 3933313 | Shadscale Scrub |
| WUPA-3833 | 470138 / 3934979 | Shadscale Scrub |
| WUPA-4116 | 471527 / 3935812 | Shadscale Scrub |
| WUPA-4676 | 474303 / 3935812 | Shadscale Scrub |
| WUPA-4727 | 474581 / 3934424 | Shadscale Scrub |
| WUPA-252 | 452366 / 3935812 | Grassland |
| WUPA-481 | 453477 / 3937201 | Grassland |
| WUPA-643 | 454310 / 3935535 | Grassland |
| WUPA-1816 | 460141 / 3934702 | Grassland |
| WUPA-1979 | 460974 / 3933313 | Grassland |
| WUPA-2040 | 461252 / 3934702 | Grassland |
| WUPA-2154 | 461807 / 3935257 | Grassland |
| WUPA-2322 | 462640 / 3935257 | Grassland |
| WUPA-2376 | 462918 / 3934702 | Grassland |
| WUPA-2595 | 464029 / 3933313 | Grassland |

provided baseline population information for various species to varying degrees, though we did not attempt any rigorous estimates of population size or density. Details of some of the sampling methods were adapted in the field (e.g. placement of traps) based on field conditions at the sites. All methods used to trap animals are approved and recommended by the American Society of Mammalogists (ASM,1987), and follow the ASM guidelines for proper treatment of animals in research.

## 3.2 Trapping

### 3.2.1 Nocturnal Small Mammals (rodents, shrews).

We primarily used Sherman live-traps (H. B. Sherman Co., 23 x 9 x 8 cm) for nocturnal small mammals. These traps are effective for most rodent species, but are relatively poor at capturing shrews. We also set out up to 10 "Tomahawk" brand cage traps for larger rodents (e.g. woodrats) and medium-sized mammals (e.g. small carnivores) in habitats appropriate for these species. Traps were deployed in one of two ways:

4. In transects, typically consisting of 10 stations spaced 15 m apart, with two traps per station, for a total of 20 traps. These transects were placed in a randomly directed line at the center of the grid cell representing the stratified random point. In targeted sampling sites, the transects were deployed to follow the habitat or feature of interest (e.g. narrow riparian area along stream courses, or the base of cliffs or rock outcrops).

5. In an irregular arrangement, based on habitat features of particular interest. This placement was only used in targeted sampling, when we were setting traps in proximity to specific microhabitat features of interest. At both monuments, we conducted some trapping that targeted woodrats, and in these cases we placed traps near woodrat nests that appeared to be active. The number of traps that we set out varied from five to 20.

We baited traps with rolled or crimped oats, or a combination of oats and peanut butter. Traps were set in the late afternoon/early evening, and checked early the following morning, so that captured animals were not exposed to the heat of the sun. In most cases, traps were only set at a particular site for one night before moving on to the next site. In a few cases (particularly with the woodrat trapping), we set traps at the same sites on two or three consecutive nights.

Small mammals that were trapped were identified to species, weighed and measured, and the age and reproductive status noted. Typical measurements included body length, tail length (with and without the terminal tuft of hairs), hind foot length, and ear length (measured from notch to tip). We took digital photographs of rare or unusual species whenever possible. Trapping effort was quantified as the number of traps set, multiplied by the number of nights the traps were open (referred to as 'trap-nights'). Any traps that were noted as non-functional when they were checked were subtracted from the total number of traps available for that night. All small mammal trapping procedures incorporated recommended precautions to minimize handler exposure to Hantavirus and other mammal-borne diseases.

### 3.2.2 Diurnal Small and Medium-Sized Mammals.

We surveyed diurnal mammals using visual searches and by trapping with Sherman traps or wire-type box traps ("Havahart," "Tomahawk"). We generally targeted trapping for diurnal mammals in specific microhabitats and favorable locations, so the arrangement was generally irregular. Traps set during the day were placed in shady spots, or were provided with artificial shade in the form of a cover board propped over the top of the trap. We checked traps set during the day at least three times over the course of the daylight hours, to prevent overheating of captured individuals. Trap effort was quantified much the same as with nocturnal trapping, but indicated as the number of 'trap-days.'

## 3.3 Visual Surveys

We conducted surveys and counts of diurnal species by walking through areas of habitat in the morning and afternoon for defined time periods (30 minutes or one hour). These surveys were purposeful searches to investigate the variety of microhabitats in the area and features that might support or attract mammals. We identified all animals seen, and noted the species, location (recorded with GPS), time of sighting, general habitat type, and specific microhabitat, as appropriate. Whenever possible, we took photos of these species using cameras equipped with telephoto lenses. Other mammal sign (tracks, scat, digging) were also recorded during these visual area surveys. In addition to standardized visual surveys, field staff also noted other diurnal mammals seen incidentally during the course of other fieldwork. Where appropriate, similar data were recorded for these 'random encounters' (date, time, species, habitat, GPS location, etc.)

## 3.4 Automatic Cameras

We used two different automatic camera systems to detect medium-sized nocturnal mammals (Wemmer et al. 1996). These included the active infrared "Trailmaster" system, which uses an infrared transmitter and receiver and a modified film camera; and the "Reconyx" system, which uses a passive infrared motion detector and an associated digital camera. Both camera systems record the date and time of each event (when the motion detector is tripped) directly on the photo. We deployed these camera units along game trails or other areas where animal traffic was funneled (e.g. in a narrow canyon or an opening in vegetation). In most cases we set out bait or scent attractants in the "viewing area" of the camera and infrared detector. Field crews usually set up camera traps in late afternoon when they arrived in an area, and left them set up for two- to four-day spans before retrieving and moving the camera to a new location.

## 3.5 Sign

We collected supplemental information on occurrence, distribution, and habitat use of small and medium-sized mammals by recording information about tracks, scat, dens, burrows and diggings. Field crews looked for mammalian sign whenever they were in the field, day or night. When they found identifiable sign, they recorded species (if this could be determined), location, habitat, and nature and condition of sign. If a particularly interesting or pertinent sign was found, it was collected, photographed (tracks, burrows), or traced onto clear acetate (tracks). We used standard identification guides (Halfpenny 1986, Murie 1974) to identify and interpret different sign that we found. Species identification was not always possible, but notes on such observations provide a useful complement to data gathered by other methods.

## 3.6 Owl Pellets

We also noted owl roosts in the vicinity of all areas that we sampled. When roosts were found, we searched for and collected pellets (the indigestible fur and bones regurgitated by the owls) from under and around the roost. These pellets were later dissected to recover bones (particularly skulls) of small mammals (Glue 1970). Owls can be effective and thorough samplers of the small mammal fauna in an area, and bones in their pellets are generally identifiable to species. Identification of these remains provided supplemental data on small and medium-sized mammals in the area. Great horned owls (*Bubo virginianus*) were the most commonly encountered owls during our surveys of the monuments. Long-eared owls (*Asio otus*) are known from WUPA and spotted owls occur at WACA. While these owl species would be good sources of mammal prey remains, we did not recover any pellets from them. We retained skulls that were in good condition for voucher purposes for the inventory.

## 3.7 Survey Methods for Bats

Because of their nocturnal nature, wide-ranging flight habits, and generally secretive roosting behavior, bats pose special challenges for inventory studies. A number of specialized survey methods are used for bats, including mist netting, harp traps, and roost surveys. However, the most cost-effective survey method, particularly for temperate North American bat species, is ultrasonic surveying of the echolocation calls emitted continuously by bats when they are active at night. Ultrasonic surveys have some important advantages over mist net surveys: (1) many bat species are difficult to capture in nets, and (2) ultrasonic recorders are not limited to use around water and other concentration areas for bats (Thomas and West 1989). Surveys using bat call recorders frequently document a range of bat species in an area when mist net surveys turn up little or nothing. In addition, ultrasonic surveys have been shown to be particularly useful for rare, widely ranging species (Drost et al. 2000, Fenton et al. 1987).

### 3.7.1 Anabat II Bat Detector

For this project, we used the Anabat II bat detector, a countdown type recorder designed specifically for identifying microchiropteran bats by the pulse rate and time pattern of the dominant frequency of their calls (Hayes and Hounihan 1994, Fenton 1988). Most of our Anabat surveys were stationary surveys with the Anabat computer system used in conjunction with mist net surveys (described below). We generally set up the computer and Anabat at or near dusk, and recorded continuously for one to four hours. The duration depended on the level of activity at the site (or lack thereof) and whether we planned to visit additional sites that evening. The person handling the Anabat typically swept it back and forth and around overhead, until calls were detected. At that point, an effort was made to "lock on" to the direction of the bat to assure that a good sequence of calls was recorded.

The recorder also used a hand-held spotlight to try to see the bat at this point. Flight patterns, and in some cases patterns of light and dark on the bat, are useful for confirming the identification of different species. To provide a permanent record of what was recorded at each site, all Anabat recordings were saved as computer files, together with notes on time, location, and species identification and behavior. In addition to facilitating identification of bats visiting an area (such as a stock tank or similar water body), the stationary surveys also permitted us to make verified reference recordings of the calls of different bat species captured in the nets. For this purpose, captured bats were released in a relatively clear, open area in front of the Anabat setup, and the person handling the Anabat kept the recorder trained on the released bat until it flew out of recording range.

We also conducted surveys from a vehicle, with one driver and one recorder handling the Anabat. These surveys incorporated real-time GPS, with UTM locations recorded for each bat species detected. Output from the Anabat was directed to a laptop computer, both for immediate display and identification of the calls, and for permanent storage to the computer hard drive. We also calculated species by species activity rates for Anabat surveys. Unless it is light enough to actually count individual bats, it is typically not possible to determine if Anabat call sequences represent many different individuals, or one or a few individuals flying back and forth

through an area. For this reason, we refer to tabulations of call sequences as measures of activity, as opposed to strict measures of abundance. For this survey, we tabulated calls separated by at least 10 minutes to produce a relative measure of activity over the course of the evening. In cases where two or more bats were definitely recorded (either visually, or in the call sequence), the additional bats within the time period were added to the total. Some bat species produce echolocation calls audible to the human ear (e.g. mastiff bat, spotted bat). Since these low-frequency calls were sometimes not recorded by Anabat (which is typically tuned for higher frequencies), we counted and tabulated these species separately as the number of bats heard, their location, and the time they were heard.

### 3.7.2 Mist Nets

We also used mist nets to capture bats at sites with open surface water in and near WACA and WUPA. Areas of water are often the only places where bats can be reliably captured in mist nets. This is particularly true in arid regions, where the bats must come to such areas to drink. At each site, we set up at least three or four mist nets along the edge of the water, or across the water, depending on the size of the water body and the amount of bat activity. We generally set up nets just before dusk, and kept them open until 10:00 to 11:00 pm. Nets were attended by one or two field crew at all times, so that bats could be removed and processed as soon as they entered the net. Captured bats were identified, sexed, and (for females) checked for reproductive condition. We recorded basic measurements, including forearm, foot, tail, and ear. We took photographs of all species captured, showing identifying characteristics whenever possible. As noted, we also released some captured individuals in front of an Anabat setup to obtain verified vocalizations. This was particularly important for some species (e.g. *Myotis* spp.) whose calls are very similar to one another. We promptly released the bats once we finished processing them.

In order to incorporate the associated data into a spatial database, we recorded mist net locations with a GPS. Summary data for each net site included general habitat features of the site (topographic position, vegetation type, presence and character of water in the vicinity), weather conditions, bat species captured, numbers, capture rate (as individuals per net hour), and breeding status of individuals captured.

Using the combined data from Anabat recordings and mist net captures we evaluated

- bat species composition in each area surveyed

- overall distribution in the parks surveyed

- relationship to habitat parameters (vegetation type, elevation, topographic position)

- seasonal occurrence patterns.

Relative abundance/activity measures were calculated separately using the Anabat recordings. Differences among sites were also tabulated for reporting purposes.

## 3.8 Voucher Specimens

We did not collect specimens from the groups we surveyed. Good quality photographs were used as vouchers for species occurrence at WACA and WUPA, in lieu of, or in addition to, existing museum study skins. We decided that good photographs (where they could be obtained) provided a more suitable means of documenting results of the inventory, especially for larger mammals and for relatively rare species.

## 3.9 Museum Searches

We reviewed published and unpublished sources for information on mammals of the study area, particularly Bateman (1976, 1980, 1981), Hoffmeister (1986), Lincoln (1961), and Salomonson (1973). We also reviewed unpublished National Park Service 'Natural History Field Observation' cards on file in the museum of the Flagstaff Monuments headquarters. These observation cards date back to the 1940s, and are a useful source of distributional and natural history information, particularly for more conspicuous species. We also reviewed mammal specimen records at the Vertebrate Museum of Northern Arizona University (NAU), and the Museum of Northern Arizona (MNA). Neither NAU nor MNA had computerized collection records,

so we went to both museums and recorded collection data directly from their card catalog into a computer database. The museum records at both institutions are organized by county, so we reviewed all records for Coconino County, Arizona, to identify specimens collected within or near WACA and WUPA. Because the mammal fauna of SUCR (located northeast of Flagstaff, between WACA and WUPA) is poorly-known, we also noted all mammal records from within and near that area.

In the tables and text that follow, taxonomy and scientific names follow Baker et al. (2003). Some of these names and taxonomic opinions differ from the National Park Service NPSpecies "master" databases, and the on-line Integrated Taxonomic Information System (ITIS; http://www.itis.usda.gov/). In the annotated appendices that follow this report, we list and explain differences in nomenclature and taxonomy, particularly if a specific name has been in common use, or has a confusing history.

# 4 Results

We conducted the majority of fieldwork for this project during spring, summer, and fall of 2002, 2003, and 2004. Also included in this report is important survey work on bats that was conducted in spring and fall of 2000. Some follow-up field surveys, specifically looking for rare diurnal small mammals (cliff chipmunk at WUPA, and spotted ground squirrel), were conducted in 2005 and 2006. Small mammal surveys sampled a combination of randomly-selected points and areas selected because of specific microhabitats of interest (i.e. "targeted surveys").

## 4.1 Sampling Effort

Over the main period of fieldwork for this study (2002 – 2004), we spent 109 person-days in the field at WACA and WUPA (person-days is calculated as the number of field personnel, times the number of full days spent on field sampling). This breaks down as 22 person-days in 2002, 14 person-days in 2003, and seven person-days in 2004 at WACA (total 43); and 22 person-days in 2002, 20 in 2003, and 24 in 2004 at WUPA (total 66). We spent

**Table 3.** Small mammal sampling effort at Walnut Canyon (WACA) and Wupatki (WUPA) National Monuments, Arizona, from 2000 through 2005. Effort is in trap nights for live traps, hours:minutes for bat sampling, and visual surveys.

| Monument | Method | Effort | Time Period | # captures | trap success |
|---|---|---|---|---|---|
| **Survey Year: 2000** | | | | | |
| WACA | Anabat / mist net | 12:38 hrs. | May-October | | |
| WUPA | Anabat | 13:56 hrs. | May-October | | |
| **Survey Year: 2002** | | | | | |
| WACA | Live traps | 480 | August-September | 36 | 7.5% |
| | Visual surveys | 44:00 hrs. | August-September | | |
| | Anabat / Mist net | 8:00 hrs. | | | |
| WUPA | Live traps | 600 | July-August | 22 | 3.7% |
| | Visual surveys | 40:00 hrs. | July – August | | |
| **Survey Year: 2003** | | | | | |
| WACA | Live traps | 650 | August-September | 42 | 6.5% |
| | Visual surveys | 84:00 hrs. | August-September | | |
| | Anabat / Mist net | 14:00 hrs. | | | |
| WUPA | Live traps | 924 | July-August | 72 | 7.8% |
| | Visual surveys | 112:00 hrs. | July-August | | |
| **Survey Year: 2004** | | | | | |
| WACA | Live traps | 360 | September-October | 26 | 7.2% |
| WUPA | Live traps | 1,042 | July-September | 154 | 14.8% |
| **Survey Year 2005** | | | | | |
| WUPA | Visual surveys | 18:00 hrs. | March - July | | |

additional time surveying for bats in 2000, and were also in the field in 2005 and 2006 on follow-up surveys for particular species of interest. Setting and checking small mammal traps at stratified random and targeted sample sites across each of the national monuments took up the greatest amount of field time. Other activities included wide-ranging visual surveys, remote camera "traps" for medium-sized nocturnal mammals, and mist-netting for bats.

Broken down by field method,

- We had a total of 4,056 trap-nights between the two monuments over the three-year period – 1,490 at WACA, and 2,566 at WUPA (Table 3).

- We had over 48 hours of night surveys for bats (mist-netting and Anabat / acoustic surveys combined; Table 3). Most of this was in 2000, when we were working with Chris Corben, an expert in using the Anabat system to conduct acoustic surveys for bats.

- We also accumulated close to 300 hours of visual surveys during this period, with 128 hours at WACA and 170 at WUPA. These general surveys took place in 2002 and 2003, with observers searching for all mammal species that were active in the survey areas. In 2005 and 2006, the surveys specifically targeted remaining mammal species that we had yet to document at the two monuments.

## 4.2 Species Diversity and Numbers

Over the course of these surveys, we recorded

**Table 4.** Numbers of mammals captured or recorded at Walnut Canyon (WACA) and Wupatki (WUPA) National Monuments, Arizona, during mammal inventory study. Symbols used are: "+" – present, numbers not recorded; "++" – numerous, numbers not recorded. Bold figures highlight the more numerous species in each group. Note: this table also includes the results of a bat survey conducted in Sunset Crater National Monument (SUCR) during the 2000 field season.

| Species | WACA | WUPA | SUCR |
|---|---|---|---|
| **Bats** | | | |
| Pallid bat (*Antrozous pallidus*) | 1 | | 2 |
| Townsend's big-eared bat (*Corynorhinus townsendii*) | | 3 | |
| Big brown bat (*Eptesicus fuscus*) | **14** | | **14** |
| Spotted bat (*Euderma maculatum*) | | 2 | |
| Allen's big-eared bat (*Idionycteris phyllotis*) | 3 | | |
| Silver-haired bat (*Lasionycteris noctivagans*) | 7 | | |
| Hoary bat (*Lasiurus cinereus*) | | | 1 |
| Southwestern myotis (*Myotis auriculus*) | 1 (near) | | |
| California myotis (*Myotis californicus*) | **21** | **10** | 2 |
| Western small-footed myotis (*Myotis ciliolabrum*) | 1 | | 1 |
| Long-eared myotis (*Myotis evotis*) | **23** | | 1 |
| Arizona myotis (*Myotis occultus*) | 4 | | |
| Fringed myotis (*Myotis thysanodes*) | **30** | **40** | 2 |
| Long-legged myotis (*Myotis volans*) | | | 1 |
| Yuma myotis (*Myotis yumanensis*) | 1 | 4 | |
| Big free-tailed bat (*Nyctinomops macrotis*) | 1 | 5 | |
| Western pipistrelle (*Pipistrellus hesperus*) | | 2 | 1 |
| Brazilian free-tailed bat (*Tadarida brasiliensis*) | 3 | 2 | 1 |
| **Medium and Large Mammals (rabbits, carnivores and ungulates; visual observations only)** | | | |
| Pronghorn (*Antilocapra americana*) | | + | |
| Coyote (*Canis latrans*) | | + | |
| Elk (*Cervus canadensis*) | + | + | |
| White-backed hog-nosed skunk (*Conepatus leuconotus*) | 2 | | |
| Bobcat (*Lynx rufus*) | 2 | 1 | |
| Striped skunk (*Mephitis mephitis*) | 2 | | |
| Mule deer (*Odocoileus hemionus*) | + | | |
| Collared peccary (*Pecari tajacu*) | 3 | | |
| Desert cottontail (*Sylvilagus audubonii*) | + | ++ | |
| American badger (*Taxidea taxus*) | | 1 | |
| Common gray fox (*Urocyon cinereoargenteus*) | 2 | | |
| American black bear (*Ursus americanus*) | 1 | | |

| Species | WACA | WUPA | SUCR |
|---|---|---|---|
| Kit fox (*Vulpes macrotis*) | | 2 | |
| **Rodents** | | | |
| White-tailed antelope squirrel (*Ammospermophilus leucurus*) | | 8 | |
| Rock pocket mouse (*Chaetodipus intermedius*) | | **39** | |
| Gunnison's prairie dog (*Cynomys gunnisoni*) | | 2 | |
| North American porcupine (*Erethizon dorsatum*) | | 2 | |
| Mogollon vole (*Microtus mogollonensis*) | 1 | | |
| Cliff chipmunk (*Neotamias dorsalis*) | 2 | 1 | |
| Western white-throated woodrat (*Neotoma albigula*) | 1 | 9 | |
| Arizona woodrat (*Neotoma devia*) | 3 | **16** | |
| Mexican woodrat (*Neotoma mexicana*) | 1 | | |
| Stephens's woodrat (*Neotoma stephensi*) | 4 | 13 | |
| Northern grasshopper mouse (*Onychomys leucogaster*) | 3 | 5 | |
| Arizona pocket mouse (*Perognathus amplus*) | | **40** | |
| Plains pocket mouse (*Perognathus flavescens*) | | 4 | |
| Silky pocket mouse (*Perognathus flavus*) | | 13 | |
| Brush mouse (*Peromyscus boylii*) | **28** | **38** | |
| Canyon mouse (*Peromyscus crinitus*) | | 9 | |
| Deer mouse (*Peromyscus maniculatus*) | **32** | 16 | |
| Pinyon mouse (*Peromyscus truei*) | **29** | **21** | |
| Western harvest mouse (*Reithrodontomys megalotis*) | 3 | 4 | |
| Abert's squirrel (*Sciurus aberti*) | + | | |
| Rock squirrel (*Spermophilus variegatus*) | 1 | 2 | |

a total of 53 species of mammals at the two monuments: 36 at WACA and 34 at WUPA. Table 4 lists numbers of each species captured, observed, or recorded (e.g. with Anabat, or with the automatic cameras). In some cases, we did not record actual numbers (e.g. with cottontails and jackrabbits, which we saw on the roads or flushed while walking to sampling sites). In these cases, the table lists either "+,"indicating the species was recorded on the monument, or "++," indicating the species was recorded, and was present in large numbers.

At both WACA and WUPA, the most frequently recorded bat was the fringed myotis (*Myotis thysanodes*) (table 4). At WACA, the next most numerous bats were long-eared myotis (*Myotis evotis*) and California myotis (*Myotis californicus*). At WUPA, California myotis followed fringed myotis as the second most numerous bat recorded.

Among rodents, three species of *Peromyscus* were most numerous in trap captures at WACA. These were (in nearly equal numbers) the deer mouse (*P. maniculatus*), pinyon mouse (*P. truei*), and brush mouse (*P. boylii*). At WUPA, two species of pocket mice were the most numerous trap captures: the Arizona pocket mouse (*Perognathus amplus*) and the rock pocket mouse (*Chaetodipus intermedius*). The next two most numerous were the brush mouse, and the pinyon mouse.

During the work in 2000, we also conducted Anabat surveys at Sunset Crater National Monument (SUCR). The bat fauna of SUCR is very poorly known. We found no museum or literature references to bat species recorded within the monument boundaries, so we have also listed these results in Table 4. We do not list numbers, or presence / absence for other mammal species at SUCR, because we did not carry out any other intensive fieldwork there. We recorded a total of ten bat species at SUCR, with the big brown bat (*Eptesicus fuscus*) being the most frequently recorded.

## 4.3 Museum Records

Our review of museum records located a total of 267 specimens of 38 species from WACA and WUPA. We recorded an additional 380 specimens that were collected within a mile or two of the boundaries of either WACA or WUPA, as well as specimens with vague locality information which did not clearly indicate if the specimen was collected inside or outside the monument. The latter specimens provided evidence that a species might possibly occur, even if we did not have other information that confirmed the species' presence within or near the monument boundaries.

Table 5 summarizes the mammal species and numbers of specimens that were collected within each of the two monuments: 19 specimens representing 19 species from WACA, and 230 specimens representing 33 different species from WUPA. Broken down by museum,

- The Museum of Northern Arizona has 47 specimens of 19 species from Walnut Canyon, and 102 specimens of 25 species from Wupatki.

- The mammal collection at the Northern Arizona University Vertebrate Museum has no mammal specimens from Walnut Canyon, but has 82 specimens representing 18 species from Wupatki.

- Other regional and national museums combined have six specimens representing three species from Walnut

Canyon, and 46 specimens of 20 species from Wupatki. The other museums with specimens from the two monuments include:

  • -the Natural History Museum of Los Angles County (LACM)

  • -the Museum of Vertebrate Zoology at the University of California at Berkeley (MVZ)

  • -the University of Arizona Museum (UA)

  • -the University of Illinois Museum of Natural History (UI)

  • -the United States National Museum of Natural History in Washington, DC (USNM)

Of these other museums, the two with the greatest number of specimens from WACA and WUPA are the University of Illinois Museum (19 specimens) and the University of Arizona Museum (21 specimens).

National Park Service 'Natural History Observation' cards provided additional specific information for the different monuments, particularly for medium-sized and large mammals. In some cases, they provided the only information available for species that were otherwise not recorded in museum records or in field surveys. One drawback of these cards is that very few of them provide any detail about how identifications were made, the certainty of the identification, or the qualifications of the observer. For this reason, we reviewed the cards carefully and critically, based on what is known of the mammal fauna of northern Arizona. Some records were clearly erroneous. For example, a short-tailed weasel was recorded on October 25, 1974 from the Bonito Lava Flow at Sunset Crater. However, short-tailed weasels are not known from Arizona, and the sighting probably refers to the long-tailed weasel (*Mustela frenata*). In another case a "mountain goat ram" was recorded for Sunset Crater on August 10, 1988, but it is not at all clear what this sighting may have referred to because the native range of mountain goats does not extend south of Idaho, and bighorn sheep were extirpated from the Sunset Crater area long before the 1980's.

*(continued on page 21)*

**Table 5.** Museum records of mammals collected from Walnut Canyon and Wupatki National Monuments, Arizona. Records are from the Museum of Northern Arizona (MNA), Northern Arizona University (NAU), and all other museums ("Other"). Many of these are cited in Hoffmeister (1986; see text, and Appendices).

| | MNA | NAU | Others |
|---|---|---|---|
| **Walnut Canyon National Monument** | | | |
| Pallid bat (*Antrozous pallidus*) | 1 | | |
| Big brown bat (*Eptesicus fuscus*) | 4 | | |
| California myotis (*Myotis californicus*) | 1 | | |
| Long-eared myotis (*Myotis evotis*) | 1 | | |
| Little brown myotis (*Myotis lucifugus*) = Arizona myotis (*M. occultus*) | 2 | | |
| Black-tailed jack rabbit (*Lepus californicus*) | 1 | | |
| Gray-collared chipmunk (*Neotamias cinereicollis*) | 3 | | |
| Cliff chipmunk (*Neotamias dorsalis*) | 4 | | |
| Abert's squirrel (*Sciurus aberti*) | 4 | | 1 |
| Golden-mantled ground squirrel (*Spermophilus lateralis*) | 5 | | |
| Rock squirrel (*Spermophilus variegatus*) | 2 | | |
| Mogollon vole (*Microtus mogollonensis*) | 2 | | |
| Mexican woodrat (*Neotoma mexicana*) | 2 | | |
| Stephens's woodrat (*Neotoma stephensi*) | 1 | | 1 |
| Brush mouse (*Peromyscus boylii*) | 3 | | 4 |
| Deer mouse (*Peromyscus maniculatus*) | 7 | | |
| Pinyon mouse (*Peromyscus truei*) | 2 | | |
| Pronghorn (*Antilocapra americana*) | 1 | | |
| Bighorn sheep (*Ovis canadensis*) | 1 | | |
| **Wupatki National Monument** | | | |
| Crawford's desert shrew (*Notiosorex crawfordi*) | 7 | 1 | |
| Pallid bat (*Antrozous pallidus*) | 5 | 2 | 1 |
| Townsend's big-eared bat (*Corynorhinus townsendii*) | | 1 | 2 |
| Silver-haired bat (*Lasionycteris noctivagans*) | | | 1 |
| California myotis (*Myotis californicus*) | | 6 | 1 |
| Western small-footed myotis (*Myotis ciliolabrum*) | | | 2 |
| Fringed myotis (*Myotis thysanodes*) | | | 2 |
| Western pipistrelle (*Pipistrellus hesperus*) | 4 | | 1 |
| Desert cottontail (*Sylvilagus audubonii*) | 2 | | |
| Black-tailed jack rabbit (*Lepus californicus*) | 5 | | |
| Cliff chipmunk (*Neotamias dorsalis*) | 1 | | |
| White-tailed antelope squirrel (*Ammospermophilus leucurus*) | 5 | | 1 |
| Spotted ground squirrel (*Spermophilus spilosoma*) | | 1 | 1 |
| Botta's pocket gopher (*Thomomys bottae*) | 3 | | |
| Silky pocket mouse (*Perognathus flavus*) | 8 | 13 | 6 |
| Arizona pocket mouse (*Perognathus amplus*) | 4 | 16 | 5 |
| Rock pocket mouse (*Chaetodipus intermedius*) | 3 | 5 | |

**Table 5. Museum records of mammals collected from Walnut Canyon and Wupatki National Monuments, Arizona, continued**

|  | MNA | NAU | Others |
|---|---|---|---|
| Ord's kangaroo rat (*Dipodomys ordii*) |  | 1 | 3 |
| Western harvest mouse (*Reithrodontomys megalotis*) | 2 | 2 | 2 |
| Deer mouse (*Peromyscus maniculatus*) | 10 | 6 | 6 |
| Canyon mouse (*Peromyscus crinitus*) | 1 | 1 | 1 |
| Brush mouse (*Peromyscus boylii*) | 1 | 2 |  |
| Pinyon mouse (*Peromyscus truei*) | 12 | 14 | 3 |
| Northern grasshopper mouse (*Onychomys leucogaster*) | 2 |  | 3 |
| Western white-throated woodrat (*Neotoma albigula*) | 4 |  | 1 |
| Arizona woodrat (*Neotoma devia*) | 5 | 1 |  |
| Stephens's woodrat (*Neotoma stephensi*) | 12 | 8 | 3 |
| North American porcupine (*Erethizon dorsatum*) | 1 |  |  |
| Coyote (*Canis latrans*) | 1 | 1 |  |
| Northern raccoon (*Procyon lotor*) | 1 |  |  |
| American badger (*Taxidea taxus*) | 1 |  | 1 |
| Western spotted skunk (*Spilogale gracilis*) |  | 1 |  |
| Bobcat (*Lynx rufus*) | 2 |  |  |

**Table 6.** Mammal species list for Walnut Canyon National Monument, Arizona, based on recent fieldwork, and review of museum data and other sources.

| Common name  (Scientific name) | Park Status |
|---|---|
| **Order Chiroptera – Bats** | |
| **Family Vespertilionidae  (vesper bats)** | |
| Pallid bat  (*Antrozous pallidus*) | Present |
| Big brown bat  (*Eptesicus fuscus*) | Present |
| Spotted bat  (*Euderma maculatum*) | Present |
| Allen's big-eared bat  (*Idionycteris phyllotis*) | Present |
| Silver-haired bat  (*Lasionycteris noctivagans*) | Present |
| Hoary bat  (*Lasiurus cinereus*) | Present |
| California myotis  (*Myotis californicus*) | Present |
| Western small-footed myotis  (*Myotis ciliolabrum*) | Present |
| Long-eared myotis  (*Myotis evotis*) | Present |
| Arizona myotis  (*Myotis occultus*) | Present |
| Fringed myotis  (*Myotis thysanodes*) | Present |
| Yuma myotis  (*Myotis yumanensis*) | Present |
| **Family Molossidae  (free-tailed bats)** | |
| Big free-tailed bat  (*Nyctinomops macrotis*) | Present |
| Brazilian free-tailed bat  (*Tadarida brasiliensis*) | Present |
| **Order Lagomorpha – Pikas, hares, and rabbits** | |
| **Family Leporidae  (hares and rabbits)** | |
| Black-tailed jackrabbit  (*Lepus californicus*) | Present |

| Common name  (Scientific name) | Park Status |
|---|---|
| Desert Cottontail  (*Sylvilagus audubonii*) | Present |
| **Order Rodentia – Rodents** | |
| **Family Sciuridae  (squirrels)** | |
| Gray-collared chipmunk  (*Neotamias cinereicollis*) | Present |
| Cliff chipmunk  (*Neotamias dorsalis*) | Present |
| Abert's squirrel  (*Sciurus aberti*) | Present |
| Golden-mantled ground squirrel  (*Spermophilus lateralis*) | Present |
| Rock squirrel  (*Spermophilus variegatus*) | Present |
| **Family Geomyidae  (pocket gophers)** | |
| Botta's pocket gopher  (*Thomomys bottae*) | Present |
| **Family Muridae  (mice, rats, and voles)** | |
| Mogollon vole  (*Microtus mogollonensis*) | Present |
| Arizona woodrat  (*Neotoma devia*) | Present |
| Mexican woodrat  (*Neotoma mexicana*) | Present |
| Stephens's woodrat  (*Neotoma stephensi*) | Present |
| Northern grasshopper mouse  (*Onychomys leucogaster*) | Present |
| Brush mouse  (*Peromyscus boylii*) | Present |
| Deer mouse  (*Peromyscus maniculatus*) | Present |
| Pinyon mouse  (*Peromyscus truei*) | Present |
| Western Harvest Mouse  (*Reithrodontomys megalotis*) | Present |
| **Family Erethizontidae  (New World porcupines)** | |
| North American porcupine  (*Erethizon dorsatum*) | Present |
| **Order Carnivora – Carnivores** | |
| **Family Canidae  (dogs, foxes, and wolves)** | |
| Coyote  (*Canis latrans*) | Present |
| Common gray fox  (*Urocyon cinereoargenteus*) | Present |
| **Family Ursidae  (bears)** | |
| American black bear  (*Ursus americanus*) | Present |
| **Family Procyonidae  (raccoons, ringtails, and coatis)** | |
| Ringtail  (*Bassariscus astutus*) | Present |
| White-nosed coati  (*Nasua narica*)[1] | Historic |
| Northern raccoon  (*Procyon lotor*) | Present |
| **Family Mustelidae  (weasels, otters, and badgers)** | |
| Long-tailed weasel  (*Mustela frenata*) | Present |
| American badger  (*Taxidea taxus*) | Present |
| **Family Mephitidae  (Skunks)** | |
| White-backed hog-nosed skunk  (*Conepatus leuconotus*) | Present |
| Striped skunk  (*Mephitis mephitis*) | Present |
| Western spotted skunk  (*Spilogale gracilis*)[2] | Present |
| **Family Felidae  (cats)** | |

*Table 6. Mammal species list for Walnut Canyon National Monument, continued*

| Common name  (Scientific name) | Park Status |
| --- | --- |
| Bobcat  (*Lynx rufus*) | Present |
| Mountain lion  (*Puma concolor*) | Present |
| **Order Artiodactyla – Even-toed ungulates** | |
| **Family Tayassuidae  (peccaries)** | |
| Collared peccary  (*Pecari tajacu*) | Present |
| **Family Cervidae  (deer)** | |
| Elk   (*Cervus canadensis*) | Present |
| Mule deer  (*Odocoileus hemionus*) | Present |
| **Family Antilocapridae  (pronghorn)** | |
| Pronghorn  (*Antilocapra americana*) | Present |
| **Family Bovidae  (cattle, antelope, sheep, and goats)** | |
| Domestic cattle (*Bos taurus*) | Non-native/Trespass |
| Bighorn sheep (*Ovis canadensis*) | Historic |

[1]Most recent records from 1958 – no evidence species is still present

[2]Reported by Salomonson (1973; as *S. putorius*), but no detail provided

**Table 7.** Mammal species list for Wupatki National Monument, Arizona, based on recent fieldwork, and review of museum data and other sources.

| Common name  (Scientific name) | Park Status |
| --- | --- |
| **Order Insectivora – Insectivores** | |
| **Family Soricidae  (shrews)** | |
| Crawford's desert shrew  (*Notiosorex crawfordi*) | Present |
| **Order Chiroptera – Bats** | |
| **Family Vespertilionidae  (vesper bats)** | |
| Pallid Bat  (*Antrozous pallidus*) | Present |
| Townsend's big-eared bat  (*Corynorhinus townsendii*) | Present |
| Big brown bat  (*Eptesicus fuscus*) | Present / Rare |
| Spotted bat  (*Euderma maculatum*) | Present |
| Silver-haired bat  (*Lasionycteris noctivagans*) | Present |
| Hoary bat  (*Lasiurus cinereus*) | Present |
| California Myotis  (*Myotis californicus*) | Present |
| Western small-footed myotis  (*Myotis ciliolabrum*) | Present |
| Fringed myotis  (*Myotis thysanodes*) | Present |
| Yuma myotis  (*Myotis yumanensis*) | Present |
| Western pipistrelle  (*Pipistrellus hesperus*) | Present |
| **Family Molossidae  (*Free-tailed Bats*)** | |
| Big free-tailed bat  (*Nyctinomops macrotis*) | Present |
| Brazilian free-tailed bat  (*Tadarida brasiliensis*) | Present |

Table 7. Mammal species list for Wupatki National Monument, continued

| Common name (Scientific name) | Park Status |
|---|---|
| **Order Lagomorpha – Pikas, hares, and rabbits** | |
| **Family Leporidae (hares and rabbits)** | |
| Black-tailed jackrabbit (*Lepus californicus*) | Present |
| Desert cottontail (*Sylvilagus audubonii*) | Present |
| **Order Rodentia – Rodents** | |
| **Family Sciuridae (squirrels)** | |
| White-tailed antelope squirrel (*Ammospermophilus leucurus*) | Present |
| Gunnison's prairie dog (*Cynomys gunnisoni*) | Present / Rare |
| Cliff chipmunk (*Neotamias dorsalis*) | Present / Rare |
| Spotted ground squirrel (*Spermophilus spilosoma*) | Present / Rare |
| Rock squirrel (*Spermophilus variegatus*) | Present |
| **Family Geomyidae (pocket gophers)** | |
| Botta's pocket gopher (*Thomomys bottae*) | Present |
| **Family Heteromyidae (pocket mice and kangaroo rats)** | |
| Rock pocket mouse (*Chaetodipus intermedius*) | Present |
| Ord's kangaroo rat (*Dipodomys ordii*) | Present |
| Arizona pocket mouse (*Perognathus amplus*)[1] | Present |
| Plains pocket mouse (*Perognathus flavescens*) | Present |
| Silky pocket mouse (*Perognathus flavus*) | Present |
| **Family Muridae (mice, rats, and voles)** | |
| Western white-throated woodrat (*Neotoma albigula*) | Present |
| Arizona woodrat (*Neotoma devia*) | Present |
| Stephens's woodrat (*Neotoma stephensi*) | Present |
| Northern grasshopper mouse (*Onychomys leucogaster*) | Present |
| Brush mouse (*Peromyscus boylii*) | Present |
| Canyon mouse (*Peromyscus crinitus*) | Present |
| Deer mouse (*Peromyscus maniculatus*) | Present |
| Pinyon mouse (*Peromyscus truei*) | Present |
| Western harvest mouse (*Reithrodontomys megalotis*) | Present |
| **Family Erethizontidae (New World porcupines)** | |
| North American porcupine (*Erethizon dorsatum*) | Present |
| **Order Carnivora – Carnivores** | |
| **Family Canidae (dogs, foxes, and wolves)** | |
| Coyote (*Canis latrans*) | Present |
| Common gray fox (*Urocyon cinereoargenteus*) | Present |
| Kit fox (*Vulpes macrotis*) | Present |
| **Family Procyonidae (raccoons, ringtails, and coatis)** | |
| Northern raccoon (*Procyon lotor*) | Present / Rare |
| **Family Mustelidae (weasels, otters, and badgers)** | |
| American badger (*Taxidea taxus*) | Present |

*Table 7. Mammal species list for Wupatki National Monument continued*

| Common name  (Scientific name) | Park Status |
| --- | --- |
| **Family Mephitidae  (skunks)** | |
| Western spotted skunk  (*Spilogale gracilis*) | Present |
| **Family Felidae  (cats)** | |
| Bobcat  (*Lynx rufus*) | Present |
| Mountain lion  (*Puma concolor*) | Present / Rare |
| **Order Artiodactyla – Even-toed ungulates** | |
| **Family Cervidae  (deer)** | |
| Elk  (*Cervus canadensis*) | Present |
| Mule deer  (*Odocoileus hemionus*) | Present |
| **Family Antilocapridae  (pronghorn)** | |
| Pronghorn  (*Antilocapra americana*) | Present |
| **Family Bovidae  (cattle, antelope, sheep, and goats)** | |
| Domestic cattle (*Bos taurus*) | Non-native / Trespass |
| Domestic sheep  (*Ovis aries*) | Non-native / Domestic |
| Goat (*Capra hircus*) | Non-native / Domestic |

[1][local subspecies is Wupatki pocket mouse, *P. amplus cineris*]

**Table 8.** Mammal species list for Sunset Crater National Monument, Arizona, based on recent fieldwork, and review of museum data and other sources.

| Common name  (Scientific name) | Park Status |
| --- | --- |
| **Order Insectivora – Insectivores** | |
| **Family Soricidae  (shrews)** | |
| Crawford's desert shrew  (*Notiosorex crawfordi*) | Present |
| **Order Chiroptera – Bats** | |
| **Family Vespertilionidae  (vesper bats)** | |
| Pallid bat (*Antrozous pallidus*) | Present |
| Big brown bat (*Eptesicus fuscus*) | Present |
| Hoary bat (*Lasiurus cinereus*) | Present |
| California myotis (*Myotis californicus*) | Present |
| Western small-footed myotis (*Myotis ciliolabrum*) | Present |
| Long-eared myotis (*Myotis evotis*) | Present |
| Fringed myotis (*Myotis thysanodes*) | Present |
| Long-legged myotis (*Myotis volans*) | Present |
| Western pipistrelle (*Pipistrellus hesperus*) | Present |
| **Family Molossidae  (free-tailed bats)** | |
| Brazilian free-tailed bat (*Tadarida brasiliensis*) | Present |
| **Order Lagomorpha – Pikas, hares, and rabbits** | |

**Table 8.** Mammal species list for Sunset Crater National Monument *continued*

| Common name  (Scientific name) | Park Status |
|---|---|
| **Family Leporidae  (hares and rabbits)** | |
| Black-tailed jackrabbit  (*Lepus californicus*) | Present |
| Desert cottontail  (*Sylvilagus audubonii*) | Present |
| **Order Rodentia – Rodents** | |
| **Family Sciuridae  (squirrels)** | |
| White-tailed antelope squirrel  (*Ammospermophilus leucurus*) | Present / Rare |
| Gray-collared chipmunk  (*Neotamias cinereicollis*) | Present |
| Cliff chipmunk  (*Neotamias dorsalis*) | Present |
| Abert's squirrel  (*Sciurus aberti*) | Present |
| Golden-mantled ground squirrel  (*Spermophilus lateralis*) | Present / Rare |
| Rock squirrel  (*Spermophilus variegatus*) | Present |
| **Family Geomyidae  (Pocket Gophers)** | |
| Botta's pocket gopher  (*Thomomys bottae*) | Present |
| **Family Muridae  (mice, rats, and voles)** | |
| Mexican woodrat  (*Neotoma mexicana*) | Present |
| Stephens's woodrat  (*Neotoma stephensi*) | Present |
| Northern grasshopper mouse  (*Onychomys leucogaster*) | Present (?) |
| Brush mouse  (*Peromyscus boylii*) | Present |
| Deer mouse  (*Peromyscus maniculatus*) | Present |
| Pinyon mouse  (*Peromyscus truei*) | Present |
| Western harvest mouse  (*Reithrodontomys megalotis*) | Present (?) |
| **Family Erethizontidae  (New World porcupines)** | |
| North American porcupine  (*Erethizon dorsatum*) | Present |
| **Order Carnivora – Carnivores** | |
| **Family Canidae  (dogs, foxes, and wolves)** | |
| Coyote  (*Canis latrans*) | Present |
| Common gray fox  (*Urocyon cinereoargenteus*) | Present |
| **Family Ursidae  (bears)** | |
| American black bear  (*Ursus americanus*) | Present / Rare |
| **Family Procyonidae  (Raccoons, Ringtails, and Coatis)** | |
| Ringtail  (*Bassariscus astutus*) | Present |
| Northern raccoon  (*Procyon lotor*) | Present |
| **Family Mustelidae  (weasels, otters, and badgers)** | |
| Long-tailed weasel  (*Mustela frenata*) | Present |
| American badger  (*Taxidea taxus*) | Present |
| **Family Mephitidae  (skunks)** | |
| Striped skunk  (*Mephitis mephitis*) | Present |
| Western spotted skunk  (*Spilogale gracilis*) | Present / Rare |
| **Family Felidae  (cats)** | |

**Table 8.  Mammal species list for Sunset Crater National Monument continued**

| Common name  (Scientific name) | Park Status |
|---|---|
| Bobcat  (*Lynx rufus*) | Present |
| Mountain lion  (*Puma concolor*) | Present |
| **Order Artiodactyla – Even-toed Ungulates** | |
| **Family Cervidae  (deer)** | |
| Elk  (*Cervus canadensis*) | Present |
| Mule deer  (*Odocoileus hemionus*) | Present |
| **Family Antilocapridae  (pronghorn)** | |
| Pronghorn  (*Antilocapra americana*) | Present |
| **Family Bovidae  (cattle, antelope, sheep, and goats)** | |
| Domestic sheep  (*Ovis aries*) | Historic |
| Bighorn sheep  (*Ovis canadensis*) | Historic |

*(continued from page 13)*

## 4.4  Species Lists

We combined the information from field surveys and from literature and museum reviews to create mammal species lists for WACA (Table 6), WUPA (Table 7), and SUCR (Table 8).

Forty-eight native mammal species, and one non-native, domestic species (cattle, occurring as occasional trespass animals) are currently known to occur at WACA. Fifteen species occur nearby in similar habitat, but no specimen records, photographs, or well-documented observations exist that place those species within or directly adjacent to monument boundaries. These species are coded as "Probably Present" or "Unconfirmed" in the National Park Service NPSpecies database, and we list them as possibly present (Appendix 3). In addition, two 'historic' species that formerly occurred at WACA (coati and bighorn sheep) have been extirpated from the region. At WUPA, a total of 48 native mammal species are documented as occurring within the monument. Three additional non-native domestic species occasionally trespass on the monument, or are allowed to graze under permit with the National Park Service (domestic cattle, sheep, and goats). At least eight other mammal species possibly occur at WUPA, but have not been documented within the boundaries of the monument (Appendix 4). Two additional species, the vagrant shrew and Abert's squirrel, have been erroneously reported at WUPA (listed as "False Report" in the NPSpecies database). The vagrant shrew record is based on a misidentified specimen of the desert shrew at the Museum of Northern Arizona. The Abert's squirrel was previously listed in error for WUPA because observation records for SUCR and WUPA had been lumped together (see Appendix 4 for further discussion).

Forty-two native mammal species are known to occur at SUCR. At least four other mammal species may occur at SUCR (Appendix 5). Two species have been documented from the monument area in historic times (bighorn sheep and the non-native domestic sheep), but are not present at this time. A record of the short-tailed weasel at SUCR is in error (evident mistake on NPS observation card, as discussed previously).

# 5  Discussion

## 5.1  Sampling Effort

This project was originally proposed for two sampling seasons, 2002 and 2003. However, it quickly became apparent in the first year that the extended drought of the time was having serious negative effects on trapping success. The annual precipitation measured at the Flagstaff Airport in 2002 was 32.72 cm

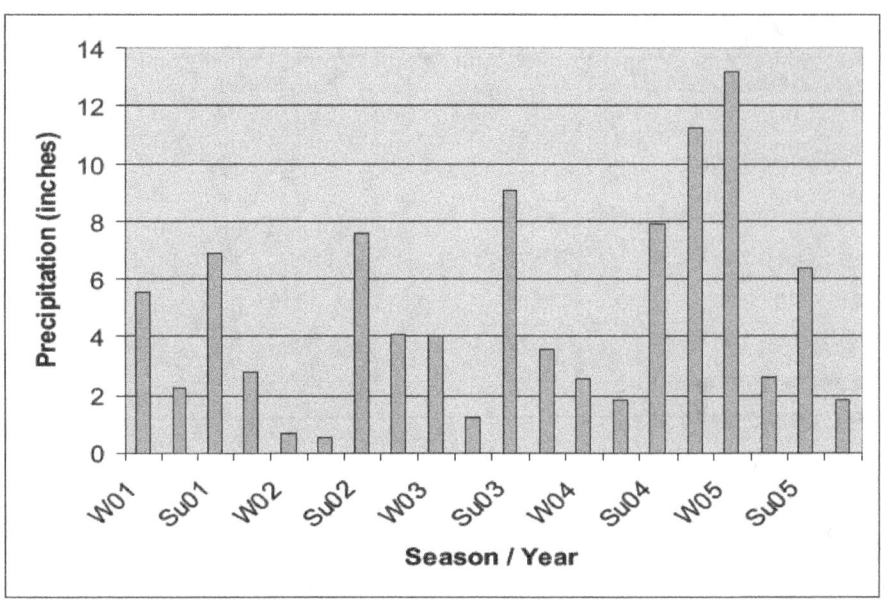

Figure 1. Quarterly precipitation for the Flagstaff area, 2000 – 2005, based on data from Flagstaff, Pulliam Airport.

(12.88 inches), compared to an annual mean of 58.19 cm (22.91 inches) (NOAA 2006). For this reason, we decided to scale back sampling to save field time and funding for better conditions. The 2003 season also had below normal precipitation of 45.34 cm (17.85 inches), though there was a good summer monsoon (fig. 1). Hence, we carried sampling over into 2004, when there was finally near-normal annual rainfall of 59.97 cm (23.61 inches). We completed small mammal live trapping with targeted efforts in 2004, but continued limited targeted visual surveys into 2005. The winter and spring of 2006 were exceptionally dry, so all fieldwork was ended at this point.

We conducted Anabat surveys at all three Flagstaff Area National Monuments, Walnut Canyon (WACA), Wupatki (WUPA), and Sunset Crater (SUCR). Most of the Anabat work was conducted in 2000, though limited Anabat surveys were also conducted in 2002 and 2003. Mist-netting was conducted in 2000, 2002, and 2003 at WACA and WUPA. Because

of habitat differences among the three monuments, our sampling strategy was different at each area. SUCR does not have any reliable areas of surface water, so we conducted Anabat surveys from a moving vehicle on the roads in and around the

monument. At WACA, Anabat surveys and mist-netting were almost all conducted around and over areas of water, including stock tanks and wastewater treatment ponds. Surveys at WUPA were carried out over or near areas of water, including Arrowhead Tank, along the south border of the monument, and along the Little Colorado River along the eastern boundary of the monument. We also surveyed at known bat roost sites, primarily at earth cracks such as Doney Fissure.

Anabat surveys are notably efficient. In about 12 ½ hours of Anabat work at WACA, we recorded nine species of bats, including six that were new for the monument, and that were only detected with Anabat (table 9). In 14 hours of Anabat surveys at WUPA, we recorded eight species of bats, including four that were new for that area. However, mist-netting was worthwhile also. Netting yielded eight species of bats at WACA, including three that were missed with Anabat: pallid bat *(Antrozous pallidus)*, hoary bat *(Lasiurus cinereus)*, and small-footed myotis *(Myotis ciliolabrum)*. All three of these are "new" for Walnut Canyon as well.

Our small mammal sampling resulted in over 4,000 trap nights of effort. Sampling sites were distributed over the entire extent and across different phases of all major habitats at both

**Table 9.** New records of mammal species for Walnut Canyon and Wupatki National Monuments, Arizona, based on fieldwork from 2000 - 2006.

| Common name  (Scientific name) | How Documented |
|---|---|
| **Walnut Canyon National Monument** | |
| Pallid bat  (*Antrozous pallidus*) | net capture |
| Big brown bat  (*Eptesicus fuscus*) | Anabat, net capture |
| Allen's big-eared bat  (*Idionycteris phyllotis*) | Anabat |
| Silver-haired bat  (*Lasionycteris noctivagans*) | Anabat |
| Hoary bat (*Lasiurus cinereus*) | net capture |
| Small-footed myotis  (*Myotis ciliolabrum*) | net capture |
| Long-eared myotis  (*Myotis evotis*) | Anabat |
| Arizona myotis  (*Myotis occultus*) | net capture |
| Fringed myotis  (*Myotis thysanodes*) | Anabat, net capture |
| Yuma myotis  (*Myotis yumanensis*) | Anabat |
| Big free-tailed bat  (*Nyctinomops macrotis*) | Anabat |
| Brazilian free-tailed bat  (*Tadarida brasiliensis*) | Anabat |
| Arizona woodrat  (*Neotoma devia*) | trap capture |
| Northern grasshopper mouse  (*Onychomys leucogaster*) | trap capture |
| Western harvest mouse  (*Reithrodontomys megalotis*) | trap capture |
| White-backed hog-nosed skunk  (*Conepatus leuconotus*) | trap capture, IR camera |
| **Wupatki National Monument** | |
| Spotted bat  (*Euderma maculatum*) | Anabat |
| Yuma myotis  (*Myotis yumanensis*) | Anabat |
| Big free-tailed bat  (*Nyctinomops macrotis*) | Anabat |
| Brazilian free-tailed bat  (*Tadarida brasiliensis*) | Anabat |
| Rock squirrel  (*Spermophilus variegatus*) | trap capture |
| Kit fox  (*Vulpes macrotis*) | visual observation |
| Common gray fox  (*Urocyon cinereoargenteus*) | visual observation |

WACA and WUPA. The selection of some sites by a stratified random procedure helped ensure that both monuments were broadly covered by our sampling efforts. We combined this with targeted sampling of important microhabitats (which were not included in the stratified random process), and sampling of specific areas that appeared suitable for "target" species (i.e. those on our preliminary hypothetical species lists that had not yet been found).

This combined sampling approach has provided a thorough assessment of the small mammal fauna at WACA and WUPA. At WUPA, we documented all of the terrestrial small mammals that were listed as "probable" species on our hypothetical species list for the area (Appendix 2) – i.e. on the mammal species list (table 7), there are no "probable" species remaining that have not been found at the monument. At WACA, the only remaining "probable" terrestrial small mammals from Appendix 1 are the Merriam's shrew (*Sorex merriami*), and three rodent species. We did not specifically sample for shrews. Because of their habits, shrews require specialized sampling techniques, such as pitfall traps, and we did not employ these techniques. The other three terrestrial small mammals that we did not find were Ord's kangaroo rat (*Dipodomys ordii*), silky pocket mouse (*Perognathus flavus*), and white-footed mouse (*Peromyscus leucopus*). All three of these species may eventually be found at WACA, but they are almost certainly rare and restricted to limited areas of suitable habitat. For example, Ord's kangaroo rat has been recorded east of Walnut Canyon, three miles northwest of Winona, and west of Walnut Canyon in Flagstaff (Hoffmeister 1986). In future surveys, Ord's kangaroo rat should be looked for in more open, lower elevations with sandy soil (e.g. in the new, eastern extension of the monument). We consider other species in Appendix 1 to be unlikely at WACA because of lack of suitable habitat and the absence of nearby records for the species.

## 5.2 Species Diversity and Numbers

Mammal species captured or otherwise documented (through Anabat recordings, photographs, etc.) at WACA and WUPA included a number of new records for each area (table 9). All of the species for SUCR may be considered "new," because this is the first

**Figure 2.** Arizona myotis (*Myotis occultus*), captured at a stock tank adjacent to Walnut Canyon National Monument. Photo courtesy of U.S. Geological Survey/Charles Drost.

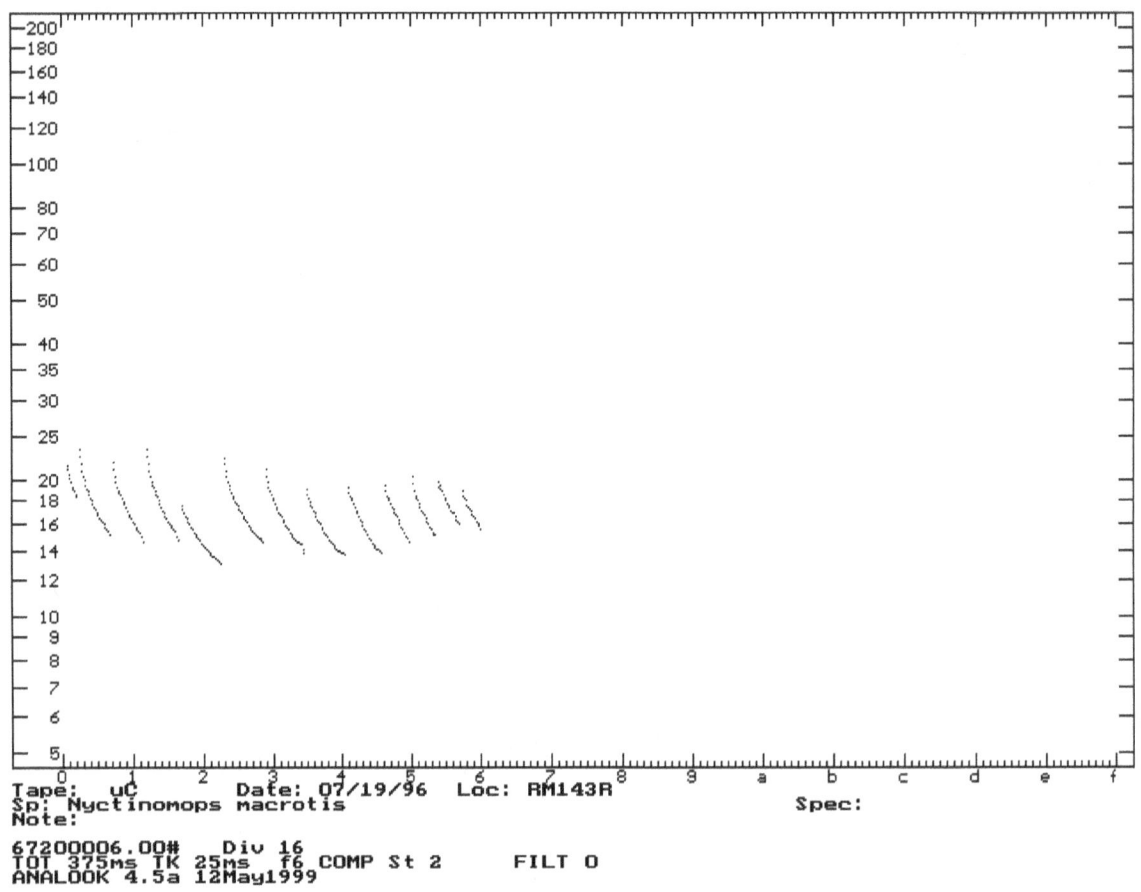

**Figure 3.** Anabat display of the call of the big free-tailed bat (*Nyctinomops macrotis*), a new record for both Walnut Canyon and Wupatki National Monument.

comprehensive list for Sunset Crater that has been carefully documented. At both WACA and WUPA, but particularly at WACA, the majority of the new records are bat species. WACA has had very little survey work for bats, and 12 of the 16 new species we documented there were bats. At WUPA, four of seven new species were bats. Most of these new records were from Anabat surveys, which identified bat species by their characteristic calls. A smaller number of the new records came from mist net captures. This new information on bats is one of the most significant contributions of the mammal surveys at WACA and WUPA. Particularly significant new records of bats for WACA include Allen's big-eared bat (*Idionycteris phyllotis*), Arizona myotis (*Myotis occultus*; fig. 2), and big free-tailed bat (*Nyctinomops macrotis*; Anabat call sequence in fig. 3). The hog-nosed skunk (*Conepatus leuconotus*; fig. 4) is also a new addition to the species list for WACA. This species appears to be moderately common at the monument, though Salomonson (1973) did not even list it as hypothetical.

At WUPA, significant additions to the known mammal fauna include the spotted bat (*Euderma maculatum*) and big free-tailed bat, with new information on roost areas of Townsend's big-eared bat (*Corynorhinus townsendii*). Judging from our daytime visual surveys, the Cliff Chipmunk (*Neotamias dorsalis*; fig. 5) is near the edge of its local range at WUPA.

Sampling for this project has also provided a better picture of some ecological aspects of small mammal communities at WACA and WUPA, such as the distribution and relative abundance of species. For example, the very localized Wupatki pocket mouse (*Perognathus amplus cineris*; fig. 6) is a subspecies of the Arizona pocket mouse and is only found in northern Arizona from the area of Wupatki National Monument north to the Echo Cliffs near Marble Canyon (Hoffmeister 1986). It is largely restricted to the Wupatki Basin in the eastern portion of the Monument, where it occurs in the saltbush desert scrub vegetation in this area. At the randomly-selected sites that we trapped at WUPA, we caught Wupatki pocket mice at six of 13 sites in Wupatki Basin (14 individuals captured), and three of five sites (eight captures) in the large canyons, such as Antelope Wash. We also caught the

**Figure 4.** Infrared automatic camera photo of a hognose skunk (*Conepatus leuconotus*), from Walnut Canyon National Monument. Photo courtesy of U.S. Geological Survey/Charles Drost.

**Figure 5.** Cliff chipmunk (*Neotamias dorsalis*); photo from near Buffalo Park, Flagstaff, AZ, courtesy of U.S. Geological Survey/Charles Drost.

species at two of 13 sites (four captures) that were designated as grassland, but one of these was at the edge of grassland and desert scrub, and the other consisted of a mix of grass and saltbush, sagebrush, and rabbitbrush.

We also found the rock pocket mouse to be more numerous and widespread at WUPA than previous studies have found. The rock pocket mouse was the second most numerous small mammal that we captured at WUPA (table 4), but it is represented by only a few captures in earlier surveys (Bateman 1980) and among museum specimens. Conversely,

**Figure 6.** The Wupatki pocket mouse (*Perognathus amplus ssp. cineris*), a restricted range variety found only at Wupatki National Monument and nearby areas. Photo courtesy of U.S. Geological Survey/Charles Drost.

**Figure 7.** An infrared automatic camera photo of a collared peccary (*Pecari tajacu*) along a game trail at Walnut Canyon National Monument. Photo courtesy of U.S. Geological Survey/Charles Drost.

we caught very few western harvest mice (*Reithrodontomys megalotis)* —none at all in 2002 and 2003, and only four in 2004; and no Ord's kangaroo rats (*Dipodomys ordii*), even though earlier studies found these species in moderate numbers. Small mammal numbers in Southwest desert habitats may vary widely from year to year, as seen in our survey results from 2002 through 2004. This may account for some of the differences in relative abundance that we saw. Likewise, differences in sampling distribution and intensity probably resulted in some differences in apparent abundance. Our results from trapping at randomly-selected sites (tables 1 and 2), should provide a fairly reliable, unbiased index of abundance of small

mammals at WACA and WUPA.

It is possible, however, that the distribution and numbers of some species are changing in response to habitat change at WUPA, particularly the increase in density and stature of grasses that has occurred since the removal of grazing from the monument, and the long-term encroachment of junipers into grassland areas in the western half of the monument. Gunnison's prairie dog (*Cynomys gunnisoni*) is one species that may be disappearing from WUPA with the loss of short grass habitat. Although there have been small colonies of this species at Wupatki in the past (see Appendix 4), we only recorded two sightings of single individual prairie dogs during the course of this project. Both were near an old prairie dog colony east of Lomaki, near the north border of the monument.

## 5.3 Museum Records

We reviewed museum records from the Museum of Northern Arizona (MNA), the Biology collections at Northern Arizona University (NAU), and several other museums that were summarized by Hoffmeister (1986). The specimen records from the two local museums (MNA and NAU) are particularly valuable for WACA and WUPA. Taken together, however, there are almost as many records from other museums combined (those summarized in Hoffmeister) as there are for the two Flagstaff museums. All of the museums with more extensive collections have some species not represented in the other museums, highlighting the value of the holdings in all of the different institutions.

We found one case of a misidentified specimen in our review of museum material. A specimen originally identified as vagrant shrew (*Sorex vagrans*[1]) from Wupatki, is in fact Crawford's desert shrew (*Notiosorex crawfordi*). There are no other records of vagrant shrew or montane shrew near Wupatki, and the species is not expected at the low elevations and arid habitats there.

During the review of museum and literature records, we frequently had to make decisions about whether the information represented

---

[1] The form in Arizona is split out as the montane shrew (*S. monticolus*) in recent references.

valid records for the three monuments. For older museum records, especially, location data for specimens is often imprecise, or just refers to a broad region. In many cases, label data listed approximate locations that are near the boundaries of the monuments, or had names of obscure historic locations. Some earlier work lumped records from the different monuments together (e.g. Lincoln 1961), and these needed to be separated out as best as possible.

One interpretation, in particular, bears discussion. The place name "Walnut" appears to have been used by Hoffmeister (1986) and possibly Salomonson (1973) as indicating Walnut Canyon. Maps in Hoffmeister place the "Walnut" location at or near Walnut Canyon National Monument, and Salomonson includes two questionable small mammal species (silky pocket mouse and plains pocket mouse [= Apache pocket mouse]) on his hypothetical list for the monument, presumably based on specimens from "Walnut." However, "Walnut" is an old name for Winona, which is about 5 km (3 miles) east of the east end of Walnut Canyon (U.S. Geological Survey 2006). Some of the collections that reference the name Walnut also note that "Walnut" is "5 miles from Turkey Tanks" or 5 miles south of Turkey Tanks. Winona is, in fact, five road miles south of Turkey Tanks.

We decided to use one mile as a cut-off for whether to accept specimen records that were near the boundaries of the three national monuments. If a record was not definitely within one mile of monument boundaries, we excluded it (or categorized the species as "Probable," if there were no other records from within a particular monument). These decisions about museum and literature data are discussed in the species accounts in the appendices. We were conservative in interpreting such information, but have strived to include it in a complete and accurate form, as these records are potentially important in understanding both the current and historic status of mammal species in each of the areas.

## 5.4 Species Lists

### 5.4.1 Walnut Canyon National Monument

We recorded 16 "new" species at WACA (table 9). These are species that were positively documented for the first time within the monument boundaries. Eleven of these were listed as "hypothetical" species by Salomonson (1973), so their occurrence was not unexpected. However, five species [Arizona myotis, Yuma myotis (*Myotis yumanensis*), big free-tailed bat, Arizona woodrat (*Neotoma devia*), and white-backed hog-nosed skunk (*Conepatus leuconotus*)] were not even considered hypothetical, so finding them at WACA was more of a surprise. Of the 16 species we found, 12 are bats, and the majority of these were detected and recorded with Anabat surveys. This large number of "new" bat species is primarily indicative of the lack of previous intensive survey for bats at WACA. Three of the other four new records of occurrence were rodents, all of which appear to be uncommon at the monument. Habitat for the grasshopper mouse and harvest mouse, in particular, is limited at WACA. The fourth species, the hog-nosed skunk, appears to be fairly common, but is inconspicuous in its nocturnal habits.

### 5.4.2 Wupatki National Monument

At WUPA, we recorded seven new species, four of which were bats (table 9). All of these were recorded with Anabat. The other three "new" species were the rock squirrel *(Spermophilus variegatus)*, the kit fox *(Vulpes macrotis)*, and the common gray fox *(Urocyon cinereoargenteus)*. Of these, the kit fox and probably the gray fox, as well, had been noted by National Park Service staff on observation cards (some card records were vague, referring to 'probable gray fox'). However, we could find no specimens or published records of either. The closest museum / literature record of kit fox to WUPA is from Merriam Crater, about 19 km to the south (Lincoln 1961; Hoffmeister 1986). WUPA is near the edge of the range of the kit fox, and the few scattered records for the area suggest that it is relatively scarce. However, we recorded one sighting and one road-killed individual during our surveys. There has been previous work on road mortality at WUPA (Persons 2001), and the effects of such mortality are potentially more consequential for rare, edge-of-range species.

### 5.4.3 Inventory Completeness

The only reasonable comparison in terms

of the completeness of this inventory study is for terrestrial small mammals and bats, as those are the only groups that we sampled intensively. At the outset of this project, we prepared a hypothetical species list, as a guide for directing the sampling effort, and also as a comparison against which to judge the resulting inventory. A significant problem with this approach, however, is that any hypothetical list is based on subjective judgments, and the hypothetical list can make the inventory list look better or worse, depending on how it was constructed. When judged against a "conservative" hypothetical list (one that only contains species that are very likely to be present in the area), the inventory list will look very good –i.e. it will score a high percentage for "completeness." In contrast, a very "liberal" hypothetical list (one containing species that are actually very unlikely to be present in the area) will make the inventory list look comparatively "bad," scoring a lower percentage of completeness. In either case, of course, neither score is demonstrably correct, because the hypothetical list was simply a best guess about the species that might occur at the site.

To try to better account for this uncertainty in the hypothetical lists, we used a weighted calculation of the species on the hypothetical list, similar to that used by Persons and Nowak (2006). Species that were already positively documented from a given area received a weight of 1. 'High-probability' species received a weight of 0.83, and 'low-probability' species received a weight of 0.17 (see Persons and Nowak 2006). We recorded a total of 30 species of bats and terrestrial small mammals at both WACA and WUPA. For WACA, the weighted hypothetical list calculation was 34.7, yielding a calculated inventory completeness of 86% [(30/34.7)*100]. For WUPA, the weighted hypothetical list calculation was 34.9. Rounded to two significant figures, this also results in an inventory completeness of 86%.

Other issues arise when trying to reduce the notion of inventory completeness to a single number. Especially among the bats, some species evidently occur within the monuments on an occasional or irregular basis. This is particularly true for relatively small areas like WACA (and even WUPA to some extent, where wide-ranging free-tailed bats probably fly into and out of the monument). The inclusion of the hoary bat for both WACA and WUPA is based on a single record for each of the monuments. Hoary bat is a migratory species and the species is not known to be resident in this area of northern Arizona, other than as spring and fall migrants. It is possible that hoary bats pass through WUPA and/or WACA on an annual basis, or they may only show up once every few years. We list hoary bat as "Present" at both monuments, but if we had missed these single brief encounters at one or both monuments, the species would have been relegated to "Probable" status.

Similar situations exist even among non-flying species. We include the cliff chipmunk on the species list for WUPA, based on a single individual seen along the south boundary fence of the monument, west of Arrowhead Sink. We specifically surveyed for this species in suitable habitats for three years (including a brief survey in spring 2006), and this was the only individual that we recorded. It is possible that a few cliff chipmunks only show up on the monument during good years, when population numbers are relatively high. At WACA, we know that White-nosed Coati (*Nasua narica*), commonly known as coatimundis, have been recorded in the past, but to our knowledge, none have been documented in the past 50 years (Salomonson 1973). Numbers of coatis appear to fluctuate widely in Arizona (Hoffmeister 1986), but there is no evidence of a current resident population (or even single individuals) in the Walnut Canyon area at present. Hence, we have noted the coati as "Historic / Extirpated" at WACA, rather than "Present."

There are other potential approaches to estimating inventory completeness using 'mark-recapture' calculations, or species-area relationships. Partly because of some of the considerations discussed above, we decided that testing, evaluation, and comparisons of such alternative approaches was more a topic for a research paper, and was beyond the scope of this report.

## 5.5 Management Considerations

Although inventories of sizeable areas are rarely fully "complete" (particularly considering changes in occurrence and numbers of some species, as discussed above), the level of sampling provided by this study—broadly distributed across the range of available habitats, over multiple years and covering a range of environmental conditions—provides a sound inventory baseline that should satisfy most requirements of natural resource managers at the Flagstaff Area National Monuments. From a management standpoint, most of the species listed as "Rare" (tables 6 and 7) or "Potential" (Appendices 3 – 5) are common, widely distributed species that are simply near the edge of their geographic and/or ecological range in these areas. As such, these species are not necessarily of special concern to Park Service managers. There are a few species—both "Present" (documented by this inventory) and "Potential" (not found, but likely to be present)—that may merit further study, and these are discussed below.

Park staff, visiting researchers, and visitors to the monuments may well be able to add to the mammal lists presented here. Interested persons should be on the lookout for those species listed as "potential species" (Appendices 3 – 5). This is particularly true of the species that are at least partly diurnal, such as long-tailed weasel at WACA. At WUPA, sightings of prairie dogs and kit foxes, in particular, are worth noting.

Mammal species of special concern at WACA and WUPA include some of the bat species and some locally-distributed small mammals. At WUPA, some of the earth cracks provide summer roosts for the Townsend's big-eared bat and other species – particularly the fringed myotis. Townsend's big-eared bat is a species of concern in many parts of the West, and is generally considered to be declining due to loss or disturbance of cave roost sites (Arizona Game and Fish Department 2003a). Some of our Anabat surveys recorded big free-tailed bats at Citadel Sink, suggesting that the cliffs there may be a roost site for this relatively rare species. We also recorded big free-tailed bat at WACA, and there is an old report of spotted bat from WACA as well. We did not conduct Anabat surveys along the rims of Walnut Canyon, but some of the cliffs within the canyon offer potential roost areas for free-tailed bats, spotted bats, and other species that utilize cracks and fissures in cliffs.

The Wupatki pocket mouse is a narrowly distributed subspecies of the Arizona pocket mouse. Its known range consists of a narrow band from the area of WUPA north to the Echo Cliffs south of Lees Ferry. Within this small range, Wupatki National Monument is the only land management area that provides long-term protection for the Wupatki pocket mouse's desert scrub habitat. This small pocket mouse has a characteristic dark pelage that matches the dark cinders and volcanic rocks in this area. Lincoln (1961) suggested that this distinctive form arose relatively recently, at the time of the cinder cone eruptions and lava flows that shaped the Wupatki landscape. As such, the Wupatki pocket mouse provides an interesting biological counterpart to the archaeological story interpreted at WUPA.

We documented the Mogollon vole (*Microtus mogollonensis*; also called the Mexican vole, *M. mexicanus*) at WACA during this study. The taxonomic status of this vole has seen changes at both the species and the subspecies level, and additional study is needed to better define relationships within the taxon. The voles from the Flagstaff area were previously grouped with those from Navajo Mountain and the south rim of Grand Canyon as the "Navajo Mexican vole" (*Microtus mexicanus navaho*; see Arizona Game and Fish Department 2003b for further discussion). This form occurs in disjunct populations within its limited range, and is listed on the State of Arizona's Wildlife of Special Concern list, and the U.S. Forest Service's Sensitive Species list (Arizona Game and Fish Department 2003b).

# 6 Literature Cited

American Society of Mammalogists. 1987. Acceptable methods in Mammalogy. Journal of Mammalogy 68(4):supplement.

Arizona Game and Fish Department. 2003a. *Corynorhinus townsendii.* Unpublished abstract compiled and edited by the Heritage Data Management System, Arizona Game and Fish Department, Phoenix, Arizona.

Arizona Game and Fish Department. 2003b. *Microtus mexicanus navaho.* Unpublished abstract compiled and edited by the Heritage Data Management System, Arizona Game and Fish Department, Phoenix, Arizona.

Armstrong, D. M., and J. K. Jones, Jr. 1971. *Sorex merriami.* Mammalian Species no. 2. American Society of Mammalogists.

Armstrong, D. M., and J. K. Jones, Jr. 1972. *Notiosorex crawfordi.* Mammalian Species no. 17. American Society of Mammalogists.

Bain, J. R. 1986. Winter roosts of Townsend's big-eared bat, *Plecotus townsendii,* (Vespertilionidae) in Wupatki National Monument and vicinity, Arizona. Unpublished report to National Park Service.

Baker, R. J., L. C. Bradley, R. D. Bradley, J. W. Dragoo, M. D. Engstrom, R. S. Hoffmann, C. A. Jones, F. Reid, D. W. Rice, and C. Jones. 2003. Revised Checklist of North American Mammals North of Mexico, 2003. Occasional Papers, Museum of Texas Tech University number 229.

Bateman, Gary C. (ed.) 1976. Natural Resource Survey and Analysis of Sunset Crater and Wupatki National Monuments, Final Report (Phase I). Report to Office of Natural Resources Management, Southwest Region, National Park Service.

Bateman, Gary C. (ed.) 1980. Natural Resource Survey and Analysis of Sunset Crater and Wupatki National Monuments, Final Report (Phase III). Report to Office of Natural Resources Management, Southwest Region, National Park Service.

Bateman, Gary C. (ed.) 1981. Natural Resource Survey and Analysis of Sunset Crater and Wupatki National Monuments, Final Report (Phase IV). Report to Office of Natural Resources Management, Southwest Region, National Park Service.

Cave Research Foundation. 1976. Wupatki National Monument earth cracks. Cave Research Foundation, Yellow Springs, Ohio.

Chung-MacCoubrey, Alice L. 2005. Use of pinyon-juniper woodlands by bats in New Mexico. Forest Ecology and Management 204: 209–220.Drost, C. A., J. Petterson, and E. Leslie. 2000. Survey of bats along the Colorado River through Grand Canyon National Park. Report to Arizona Game and Fish Department, Heritage Grant no. I96031

Drost, C. A., J. Petterson, and E. Leslie. 2000. Survey of bats along the Colorado River through Grand Canyon National Park. Report to Arizona Game and Fish Department, Heritage Grant no. I96031.

Fenton, M. B., D. C. Tennant, and J. Wyszecki. 1987. Using echolocation calls to measure the distribution of bats: the case of *Euderma maculatum.* Journal of Mammalogy. 68:142-144.

Fenton, M. B. 1988. Detecting, recording, and analyzing vocalizations of bats. pp. 91-104 in: T. H. Kunz (ed.), Ecological and behavioral methods for the study of bats. Smithsonian Institution Press, Washington, DC.

Fenton, M. B., and G. P. Bell. 1981. Recognition of species of insectivorous bats by their echolocation calls. Journal of Mammalogy 62(2):233-243.

Glue, David E. 1970. Avian predator pellet analyses and the mammalogist. Mammal Review 1:53-62.

Halfpenny, James. 1986. A field guide to mammal tracking in North America. Johnson Books, Boulder, Colorado.

Hansen, Monica, Janet Coles, Kathryn A. Thomas, Daniel Cogan, Marion Reid, Jim Von Loh, and Keith Schulz. 2004. USGS-NPS National Vegetation Mapping Program: Sunset Crater Volcano National Monument, Arizona, Vegetation Classification and Distribution. Final Report to USGS-NPS National Vegetation Mapping Program. U.S. Geological Survey, Southwest Biological Science Center.

Hayes, J. P., and P. Hounihan. 1994. Field use of the Anabat II bat-detector system to monitor bat activity. Bat Research News 35: 1-3.

Hoffmeister, Donald F. 1986. Mammals of Arizona. University of Arizona Press, Tucson, Arizona.

Jones, C., W. J. McShea, M. J. Conroy, and T. H. Kunz. 1996. Capturing mammals. Pp. 115-155 in: D. E. Wilson, F. C. Cole, J. D. Nichols, R. Rudran, and M. S. Foster (eds.), Measuring and monitoring biological diversity: standard methods for mammals. Smithsonian Press, Washington, D.C.

Kaufmann, J. H., D. V. Lanning, and S. E. Poole. 1976. Current status and distribution of the coati in the United States. Journal of Mammalogy 57: 621-637.

Lincoln, Edward P. 1961. A comparative study of present and past mammalian fauna of the Sunset Crater and Wupatki areas of northern Arizona. M. S. Thesis, University of Arizona.

McCutchen, H. E. 1995. Desert bighorn sheep. Pages 333–336 in E. T. LaRoe, G. S. Farris, C. E. Puckett, P. D. Doran, and M. J. Mac, editors. Our living resources: Abundance, and health of U.S. plants, animals, and ecosystems. U.S. Department of the Interior, National Biological Service, Washington, D.C.

Mikesic, David G., and Charles T. LaRue. 2003. Recent status and distribution of red foxes (*Vulpes vulpes*) in northeastern Arizona and southeastern Utah. Southwestern Naturalist 48: 624-634.

Murie, Olaus J. 1974. A field guide to animal tracks. Houghton Mifflin Co., Boston, Massachusettes.

National Oceanic and Atmospheric Administration (NOAA). 2006. Climatography of the United States, no. 20, Flagstaff Pulliam AP, AZ, 1971-2000. Available on the web at: www.ncdc.noaa.gov/oa/climate/normals/usnormals.html.

National Park Service (NPS). 2002a. Final Environmental Impact Statement / General Management Plan, Wupatki National Monument, Arizona. U.S. Department of the Interior, National Park Service.

National Park Service (NPS). 2002b. General Management Plan / Final Environmental Impact Statement, Sunset Crater Volcano National Monument, Arizona. U.S. Department of the Interior, National Park Service.

National Park Service (NPS). 2003. Draft Environmental Impact Statement / General Management Plan, Walnut Canyon National Monument, Arizona. U.S. Department of the Interior, National Park Service.

National Park Service (NPS). 2007. Final Environmental Impact Statement / Final General Management Plan, Walnut Canyon National Monument, Arizona. U.S. Department of the Interior, National Park Service.

Persons, Trevor B. 2001. Distribution, activity, and road mortality of amphibians and reptiles at Wupatki National Monument, Arizona. Final report to National Park Service, Flagstaff Areas National Monuments, Colorado Plateau Field Station, Flagstaff, Arizona.

Persons, Trevor B, and Charles A. Drost. 2001. Mapping and biological reconnaissance of earth crack and blowhole features at Wupatki National Monument, Arizona Final report to National Park Service, Flagstaff Areas National Monuments. Colorado Plateau Field Station, Flagstaff, Arizona.

Persons, Trevor B., and Erika M. Nowak. 2006. Inventory of Amphibians and Reptiles in Southern Colorado Plateau National Parks. U.S. Geological Survey, Southwest Biological Science Center, Colorado Plateau Research Station, Open File Report 2006-1132.

Reid, Fiona A. 2006. A field guide to mammals of North America north of Mexico. Houghton Mifflin Co., Boston, Massachusettes.

Salomonson, Michael G. 1973. The Mammals of Walnut Canyon National Monument. Plateau 46: 19-24.

Salomonson, Michael G. 1985. A checklist of mammals of Walnut Canyon National Monument. Southwest Parks and Monuments Association, Tucson, Arizona.

Stohlgren, T. J., and J. F. Quinn., 1992. An assessment of biotic inventories in western U. S. National Parks. Natural Areas Journal 12(3): 145-154.

Streubel, D. P., and J. P. Fitzgerald. 1978. *Spermophilus spilosoma*. Mammalian Species no. 101. American Society of Mammalogists.

Stuart, Maureen. 2000. Biological inventory of National Park areas on the southern Colorado Plateau. Proposal for the National Park Service Inventory and Monitoring Office.

Thomas, D. W., and S. D. West. 1989. Sampling methods for bats. Gen. Tech. Rep. PNW-GTR-243. Portland, OR: USDA Forest Service, Pacific Northwest Research Station, 20 pp.

U.S. Geological Survey. 2006. U.S. Board on Geographic Names (available online at http://geonames.usgs.gov/pls/gnispublic).

van Riper, Charles, and Richard Ockenfels. 1998. The influence of transportation corridors on the movement of Pronghorn Antelope over a fragmented landscape in northern Arizona. Proceedings of the International Conference on Ecology and Transportation, Fort Myers, Florida.

Wallmo, O. C., and S. Gallizioli. 1954. Status of the coati in Arizona. Journal of Mammalogy 35: 48-54.

Wemmer, C., T. H. Kunz, G. Lundie-Jenkins, and W. J. McShea. 1996. Mammalian sign. Pp. 157-176 in: D. E. Wilson, F. C. Cole, J. D. Nichols, R. Rudran, and M. S. Foster (eds.), Measuring and monitoring biological diversity: standard methods for mammals. Smithsonian Press, Washington, D.C.

Wetherill, M. A. 1957. Occurrence of coati in northern Arizona. Journal of Mammalogy 38: 123.

# Appendix 1

## Hypothetical mammal species list for Walnut Canyon National Monument, Arizona.

This list was prepared at the outset of an inventory study conducted from 2002 – 2006, and served as a guide for targeting field sampling and as a point of comparison for inventory completeness.

**Family Soricidae**
> Desert shrew  (*Notiosorex crawfordi*)
> Merriam's shrew  (*Sorex merriami*)

**Family Vespertilionidae**
> Pallid bat  (*Antrozous pallidus*)
> Big brown bat  (*Eptesicus fuscus*)
> Spotted bat  (*Euderma maculatum*)
> Allen's lappet-browed bat  (*Idionycteris phyllotis*)
> Townsend's big-eared bat  (*Corynorhinus townsendii*)
> Silver-haired bat  (*Lasionycteris noctivagans*)
> Hoary bat  (*Lasiurus cinereus*)
> Western pipistrelle  (*Pipistrellus hesperus*)
> California myotis  (*Myotis californicus*)
> Long-eared myotis  (*Myotis evotis*)
> Small-footed myotis  (*Myotis ciliolabrum*)
> Little brown myotis  (*Myotis lucifugus*)
> Fringed myotis  (*Myotis thysanodes*)
> Long-legged myotis  (*Myotis volans*)
> Yuma myotis  (*Myotis yumanensis*)

**Family Molossidae**
> American free-tailed bat  (*Tadarida brasiliensis*)

**Family Erethizontidae**
> Porcupine  (*Erethizon dorsatum*)

**Family Heteromyidae**
> Ord's kangaroo rat  (*Dipodomys ordii*)
> Rock pocket mouse  (*Perognathus intermedius*)
> Plains pocket mouse  (*Perognathus flavescens*)  [=Apache p. mouse  (*P. apache*)]
> Silky pocket mouse  (*Perognathus flavus*)

**Family Muridae**
> Mexican vole  (*Microtus mexicanus*)  [= Mogollon Vole  (*Microtus mogollonensis*)]
> White-throated wood rat  (*Neotoma albigula*)
> Mexican wood rat  (*Neotoma mexicana*)
> Stephens's wood rat  (*Neotoma stephensi*)
> Northern grasshopper mouse  (*Onychomys leucogaster*)
> Brush mouse  (*Peromyscus boylii*)

**Family Muridae (*continued*)**

Canyon mouse (*Peromyscus crinitus*)

Deer mouse (*Peromyscus maniculatus*)

Pinyon mouse (*Peromyscus truei*)

Western harvest mouse (*Reithrodontomys megalotis*)

**Family Geomyidae**

Botta's pocket gopher (*Thomomys bottae*)

**Family Sciuridae**

White-tailed antelope squirrel (*Ammospermophilus leucurus*)

Gunnison's prairie dog (*Cynomys gunnisoni*)

Gray-collared chipmunk (*Tamias cinereicollis*)

Cliff chipmunk (*Tamias dorsalis*)

Abert's squirrel (*Sciurus aberti*)

Golden-mantled squirrel (*Spermophilus lateralis*)

Rock squirrel (*Spermophilus variegatus*)

**Family Leporidae**

Black-tailed jack rabbit (*Lepus californicus*)

Desert cottontail (*Sylvilagus audubonii*)

**Family Canidae**

Coyote (Canis latrans)

Gray fox (Urocyon cinereoargenteus)

**Family Ursidae**

Black bear (*Ursus americanus*)

**Family Procyonidae**

Ringtail (*Bassariscus astutus*)

Coati (*Nasua narica*)

Raccoon (*Procyon lotor*)

**Family Mustelidae**

Long-tailed weasel (*Mustela frenata*)

Badger (*Taxidea taxus*)

**Family Mephitidae**

Hog-nosed skunk (*Conepatus mesoleucus*)

Striped skunk (*Mephitis mephitis*)

Western spotted skunk (*Spilogale gracilis*)

**Family Felidae**

Mountain lion (*Puma concolor*)

Bobcat (*Lynx rufus*)

**Family Antilocapridae**

Pronghorn (*Antilocapra americana*)

### Family Cervidae

Elk, or wapiti  (*Cervus elaphus*)

Mule deer  (*Odocoileus hemionus*)

### Family Tayassuidae

Collared peccary  (*Tayassu tajacu*)  [= *Pecari tajacu*]

# Appendix 2

**Hypothetical mammal species list for Wupatki National Monument, Arizona.**

This list was prepared at the outset of an inventory study conducted from 2002 - 2006, and served as a guide for targeting field sampling, and as a point of comparison for inventory completeness.

| Common Name | Scientific Name | Notes |
|---|---|---|
| **Family Soricidae** | | |
| Desert shrew | *Notiosorex crawfordi* | Hoffmeister 1986, Museum |
| **Family Vespertilionidae** | | |
| Yuma myotis | *Myotis yumanensis* | Possible at WUPA, but not documented there |
| Long-eared myotis | *Myotis evotis* | Lincoln (1961) suggests possible occurrence at WUPA, but no documentation |
| Fringed myotis | *Myotis thysanodes* | Checklist, Museum, Hoffmeister 1986;  status? |
| Long-legged myotis | *Myotis volans* | Lincoln (1961) suggests possible occurrence at WUPA |
| California myotis | *Myotis californicus* | Museum, Hoffmeister 1986; current status not known |
| Small-footed myotis | *Myotis leibii* | Checklist, Museum, Hoffmeister 1986; current status unknown |
| Western pipistrelle | *Pipistrellus hesperus* | Museum, Hoffmeister 1986; WUPA status not known |
| Big brown bat | *Eptesicus fuscus* | Checklist; status at WUPA not known |
| Western red bat | *Lasiurus blossevilli* | Expected by Lincoln (1961) at WUPA, only in migration |
| Hoary bat | *Lasiurus cinereus* | Expected at WUPA by Lincoln, but would only occur in migration |
| Townsend's big-eared bat | *Plecotus townsendii* | Museum, Salomonson 1973 |
| Allen's big-eared bat | *Idionycteris phyllotis* | Possible at WUPA; not documented |
| Pallid bat | *Antrozous pallidus* | Museum; current status at WUPA not known |
| **Family Molossidae** | | |
| Mexican free-tailed bat | *Tadarida brasiliensis* | Expected at WUPA by Lincoln (1961) |
| **Family Leporidae** | | |
| Desert cottontail | *Sylvilagus audubonii* | Checklist, Museum, Hoffmeister 1986 |
| Black-tailed jack rabbit | *Lepus californicus* | Checklist, Museum, Hoffmeister 1986 |
| **Family Sciuridae** | | |
| Cliff chipmunk | *neotamias dorsalis* | |
| White-tailed antelope squirrel | *Ammospermophilus leucurus* | Museum, Hoffmeister 1986 |
| Spotted ground squirrel | *Spermophilus spilosoma* | Museum, Hoffmeister 1986; rare |
| Rock squirrel | *Spermophilus variegatus* | Museum records; ? |
| Gunnison's prairie dog | *Cynomys gunnisoni* | Hoffmeister 1986. Known in WUPA near Lomaki |
| **Family Geomyidae** | | |
| Botta's pocket gopher | *Thomomys bottae* | Checklist, Museum, Hoffmeister 1986 |
| **Family Heteromyidae** | | |
| Plains pocket mouse | *Perognathus flavescens* | Checklist, Museum, Hoffmeister 1986 |
| Silky pocket mouse | *Perognathus flavus* | Checklist, Museum, Hoffmeister 1986 |
| Arizona pocket mouse | *Perognathus amplus* | Museum, Hoffmeister 1986 |
| Rock pocket mouse | *Perognathus intermedius* | Museum, Hoffmeister 1986 |
| Ord's kangaroo rat | *Dipodomys ordii* | Checklist, Museum, Hoffmeister 1986 |

| Common Name | Scientific Name | Notes |
| --- | --- | --- |
| **Family Muridae** | | |
| Deer mouse | *Peromyscus maniculatus* | Museum, Hoffmeister 1986 |
| Canyon mouse | *Peromyscus crinitus* | Hoffmeister 1986; Wupatki Pueblo |
| Brush mouse | *Peromyscus boylii* | Hoffmeister 1986, Museum |
| Pinyon mouse | *Peromyscus truei* | Checklist, Museum, Hoffmeister 1986 |
| Northern grasshopper mouse | *Onychomys leucogaster* | Checklist, Museum, Hoffmeister 1986 |
| White-throated woodrat | *Neotoma albigula* | Checklist, Museum, Hoffmeister 1986 |
| Arizona woodrat | *Neotoma devia* | Museum, Hoffmeister 1986; formerly lumped with N. lepida |
| Stephens's woodrat | *Neotoma stephensi* | Checklist, Museum, Hoffmeister 1986 |
| Mexican woodrat | *Neotoma mexicana* | not likely at WUPA |
| **Family Erethizontidae** | | |
| Porcupine | *Erethizon dorsatum* | Checklist, Museum |
| **Family Canidae** | | |
| Coyote | *Canis latrans* | Museum |
| Kit fox | *Vulpes macrotis* | Museum, Hoffmeister 1986; WUPA has old skull from Merriam Crater. |
| Gray Fox | *Urocyon cinereoargenteus* | Checklist, Museum |
| **Family Ursidae** | | |
| Black bear | *Ursus americanus* | status at WUPA? |
| **Family Procyonidae** | | |
| Ringtail | *Bassariscus astutus* | status at WUPA? |
| **Family Mustelidae** | | |
| Long-tailed weasel | *Mustela frenata* | not documented from WUPA |
| Badger | *Taxidea taxus* | Museum, Hoffmeister 1986, sight records |
| **Family Mephitidae** | | |
| Spotted skunk | *Spilogale gracilis* | Museum specimen from 1 mi. S of WUPA boundary on 545 |
| Striped skunk | *Mephitis mephitis* | Checklist; no specimens from WUPA; status not certain |
| **Family Felidae** | | |
| Mountain lion | *Felis concolor* | ranges near WUPA, but not documented from within monument |
| Bobcat | *Lynx rufus* | Checklist, Museum, Hoffmeister 1986. |
| **Family Cervidae** | | |
| Elk, or wapiti | *Cervus elaphus* | Checklist; rare at WUPA |
| Mule deer | *Odocoileus hemionus* | |
| **Family Antilocapridae** | | |
| Pronghorn | *Antilocapra americana* | Checklist, Museum, Hoffmeister 1986 |
| **Family Bovidae** | | |
| Sheep | *Ovis aries* | Permitted grazing in Wupatki Basin |
| Cow | *Bos taurus* | Probably casual trespass visitor to all three monuments |

# Appendix 3

## Annotated mammal species list for Walnut Canyon National Monument, Arizona.

Information provided for each species includes presence or absence within the Monument, documentation (e.g. museum specimens, trap capture, or sightings), and what is known of the species' distribution and abundance. Museum abbreviations include: MNA – Museum of Northern Arizona; NAU – Northern Arizona University Vertebrate Museum; UI – University of Illinois Museum; and USNM – United States National Museum.

## Order Chiroptera – Bats

### Family Vespertilionidae – Vesper bats

Pallid bat (*Antrozous pallidus*) – We recorded a single individual pallid bat at WACA during Anabat surveys, and captured two additional individuals during mist-netting at the monument. A single specimen of pallid bat, collected from Walnut Canyon, is housed at MNA.

Big brown bat (*Eptesicus fuscus*) – The big brown bat was one of the most common bats we recorded during our surveys at Walnut Canyon. We captured six individuals in mist nets, and recorded 23 call sequences of big brown bats with Anabat, which we judged to represent at least 14 individuals. Four big brown bats were also mist-netted at the sewage ponds in 1973 and 1974. Individuals were also identified roosting in rock crevices during the same time period. The Museum of Northern Arizona has four specimens of big brown bat collected from Walnut Canyon.

Spotted bat (*Euderma maculatum*) – The spotted bat has been recorded at Walnut Canyon in the past, but we did not detect it during our surveys – either with Anabat or mist-netting. Spotted bats are very wide-ranging during their night-time foraging, and likely are present at Walnut Canyon as occasional transients (though some could roost in the high cliffs within Walnut Canyon. The museum for the Flagstaff Area National Monuments had a spotted bat specimen at one time, but this has been lost.

Allen's big-eared bat (*Idionycteris phyllotis*) – This species is called 'Allen's lappet-browed bat' by Hoffmeister (1986). Allen's big-eared bat was recorded for the first time during Anabat and mist net surveys at the sewage ponds north of the visitor center / housing area at Walnut Canyon. Seven of the relatively low-pitched call sequences of this species were recorded, and individuals were seen flying relatively low (4 – 5 m high) along the edge of the pines surrounding the ponds. Allen's big-eared bat has been most often recorded in areas of ponderosa pine (Hoffmeister 1986), and several individuals have been collected in the area just north and northwest of Flagstaff (MNA specimens), so their presence at Walnut Canyon is not surprising. The nearest museum records that we found of this species in proximity to Walnut Canyon were from "SW base of Mt. Elden, Flagstaff" (2 individuals – NAU, 10 July 1968).

Silver-haired bat (*Lasionycteris noctivagans*) – We recorded this species with Anabat and also captured one individual in a mist net. These are the first records for silver-haired bat within the boundaries of Walnut Canyon, but the species appears to be fairly common there. With Anabat, we recorded 23 call sequences judged to represent at least seven individuals. These Anabat records were from the sewage ponds at the north end of the visitor center / housing area, and from Log Cabin Tank, along the south side of the Old Walnut Canyon Road, north of the west end of the monument. The one individual that we captured was at Onyx Tank, about 1.8 km east of Santa Fe Dam. The nearest museum specimen we found was from "Pond at head of Rio de Flag, MNA grounds, 3 mi N of Flagstaff" (MNA, 16 July 1969). The silver-haired bat is a denizen of coniferous forests and adjacent openings (Hoffmeister 1986), such as those found at Walnut Canyon.

Hoary bat (*Lasiurus cinereus*) – We captured a single individual hoary bat at Onyx Tank on 4 September 2002. Onyx Tank is about 1.8 km east of Santa Fe Dam, south of the east end of the new extension of Walnut Canyon NM. Hoary bats are migratory, with larger numbers passing through our area on their spring and fall migrations. There are relatively few records of hoary bat in northern Arizona (Hoffmeister 1986, and records at MNA). We do not know whether this is a true reflection of their relative rarity, or simply a result of the difficulty of detecting them (or perhaps a combination of the two factors). The nearest museum record we found to Walnut Canyon was from "3.75 mi N of Old Hwy 66, Turkey Tank" (assumed to be north of Winona; NAU, 19 August 1967).

California myotis (*Myotis californicus*) – In our Anabat surveys in and around Walnut Canyon, we recorded 64 call sequences of California myotis, judged to represent at least 22 individuals. These were recorded at the sewage ponds north of the visitor center/housing area at the monument, and at Log Cabin Tank, north of the west end (new addition) of the monument. There is also an observation card record from 1972 of a single California myotis captured out of a crevice in a rock wall. A single specimen of California myotis has been collected from Walnut Canyon. This specimen is housed at the Museum of Northern Arizona.

Western small-footed myotis (*Myotis ciliolabrum*) – Older references treat this species under the name *M. leibii* (e.g. Hoffmeister 1986) or *M. subulatus* (e.g. Burt and Grossenheider 1976). Formerly, it was thought that there was one 'small-footed myotis' that occurred across North America. It is now recognized that there are two species – an eastern form (M. leibii) and a western form (M. ciliolabrum). We captured (and subsequently recorded with Anabat, on release) a single individual of western small-footed myotis at the sewage ponds just north of the visitor center / housing area at Walnut Canyon. The nearest museum specimens we found were from the Southwest base of Mt. Elden, Flagstaff (NAU, 23 June 1968) and from the Northern Arizona University campus (NAU, 30 July 1979).

Long-eared myotis (*Myotis evotis*) – A single long-eared myotis was mist-netted at the sewage ponds north of the visitor center / housing area on 19 July 1973 (NPS natural history observation card). Judged in terms of level of acoustic activity, this is one of the more common Myotis species at Walnut Canyon. We recorded 86 call sequences in Anabat surveys at the sewage ponds north of the visitor center / housing area on 13 May 2000. The long-eared myotis was noted as the "most common bat present later in evening" at Log Cabin Tank on 12 May 2000. Other of the many unidentified calls in the 40 kilohertz range may also have been this species. The long-eared myotis is a species of the ponderosa and spruce-fir forests in Arizona, so its prominence in our surveys is not surprising. One specimen of long-eared myotis (now housed at MNA) had been collected previously from Walnut Canyon.

Arizona myotis (*Myotis occultus*) – The Arizona myotis has been considered to be conspecific with the widespread little brown myotis *(Myotis lucifugus)* by some authors. Hoffmeister (1986) provides a good summary of the taxonomic history of this form, along with an analysis suggesting that it is a distinct species from M. lucifugus. Baker et al. (2003) and Reid (2006) both list it as separate from *M. lucifugus*. We caught two individuals of Arizona myotis in our mist-netting, at Onyx Tank and Jesse's Tank (both southeast of the monument). Two Arizona myotis were also mist-netted at the sewage ponds north of the visitor center / housing area on 19 July 1973 (NPS natural history observation card; species listed as M. lucifugus). We did not definitely record this species with Anabat, but we did record many unidentified Myotis species with calls in the 40 kilohertz range (over 230), and some of these may have been Arizona myotis. Bats with calls in this frequency range could be a combination of Myotis ciliolabrum, Myotis evotis and Myotis occultus, all of which are known from Walnut Canyon. The Museum of Northern Arizona has two specimens of Arizona myotis collected from Walnut Canyon.

Fringed myotis (*Myotis thysanodes*) – We mist-netted a single fringed myotis at Onyx Tank on 4 September 2002, and recorded calls of the species at the Walnut Canyon sewage ponds on 13 May 2000 and at Log Cabin Tank on 15 October 2000. At the sewage ponds, 33 call sequences recorded may have represented at least 16 individuals. The nearest museum specimens of this species to Walnut Canyon are from "WSW Base of Mt. Elden" (NAU, 10 July 1968). There is (or was formerly) a colony of fringed myotis in a potato cellar on the grounds of the Museum of Northern Arizona (MNA specimens, 13 August 1968).

Yuma myotis (*Myotis yumanensis*) – We recorded Yuma myotis during Anabat surveys at Log Cabin Tank on 15 October 2000. This species characteristically forages low over the water of ponds and calmer areas of flowing waters. There are no museum specimen records from very close to Walnut Canyon (the nearest record we could find was from "Slide Rock, Oak Creek, 10 mi N of Sedona" – MNA, 19 July 1969), though we also recorded Yuma myotis at Wupatki NM during our surveys.

### Family Molossidae – Free-tailed bats

Big free-tailed bat (*Nyctinomops macrotis*) – Two sequences of the low-frequency calls of the big free-tailed bat were recorded over Log Cabin Tank on 15 October 2000. This wide-ranging species is evidently an occasional visitor to Walnut Canyon. It typically roosts in crevices in high cliffs, so it is possible that one or more roosts may be present in the cliff walls of Walnut Canyon. There are no museum specimen records from anywhere near Walnut Canyon, but this is not surprising as this is a comparatively rare (though widely ranging) species.

Brazilian Free-tailed Bat (*Tadarida brasiliensis*) – This species is more commonly known as the Mexican free-tailed bat, but both Baker et al. (2003) and Reid (2006) use the name 'Brazilian free-tailed bat,' following the species portion of the scientific name. We recorded ten call sequences of Brazilian free-tailed bats at the sewage ponds north of the visitor center / housing area on 13 May 2000, and at Log Cabin Tank on 15 October 2000. This is a wide-ranging species that typically roosts in moderate-sized to very large colonies in caves, buildings, and similar sites. There may be free-tailed bat roosts in the cliffs of Walnut Canyon, or the bats at the monument may be flying in from roosts in surrounding areas. The nearest museum specimen that we could find was from "10.5 mi S & 3 mi W of Flagstaff" (NAU, 15 July 1968). This is rather surprising insofar as this species is common in the Flagstaff area, with thousands having been documented roosting in some buildings on the Northern Arizona University campus.

## Order Lagomorpha – Pikas, hares, and rabbits

### Family Leporidae – Hares and rabbits

Black-tailed jackrabbit (*Lepus californicus*) – Black-tailed jackrabbits are present at Walnut Canyon NM, but they are evidently uncommon. We did not record any jackrabbits during our field surveys, but we did not conduct any surveys specifically for lagomorphs. Descriptions on NPS natural history observation cards range from "common" to "rare." There is one specimen of black-tailed jackrabbit from "Walnut Canyon Nat'l Mon." collected by Milton Wetherill (MNA, 02/16/1937).

Desert cottontail (*Sylvilagus audubonii*) – Desert cottontails are present in suitable habitat at Walnut Canyon, and are reported to be "common" in places. We photographed two individuals with automatic infrared camera setups – one in the canyon bottom about 250 m east of Santa Fe Dam on 29 September 2004, and one in the canyon bottom near the confluence of Cherry Canyon and Walnut Canyon on 19 October 2004. NPS natural history observation card records from 1951 through 1971 describe desert cottontail as "common" to "very common." These descriptions may in part reflect the numbers of cottontails on lawn areas, grassy roadside margins, and other favorable habitats modified by humans, in the visitor center and residence areas where most of the observations were noted. The nearest museum specimen of desert cottontail to Walnut Canyon is from "1 mi E of Sunset Crater" (MNA, 12 January 1969).

## Order Rodentia – Rodents

### Family Sciuridae – Squirrels

Gray-collared chipmunk (*Neotamias cinereicollis*) – The western chipmunks have variously been placed in the genera *Tamias* and *Eutamias*. Recent taxonomic studies, including genetic analyses, point toward recognizing three different groups of chipmunks, with *Tamias* used for the eastern chipmunk, and *Neotamias* for all western U.S. chipmunks (Baker et al 2003; but also see Reid 2006, who uses *Tamias* for western chipmunks). In addition to changes in the genus name, there has been past confusion regarding the species *N. cinereicollis*. Earlier records of striped chipmunks seen and collected in and around Walnut Canyon referred to them variously as *hopiensis* and *quadrivittatus*. Neither the Hopi chipmunk (*N. hopiensis* – now given the name *N. rufus* by both Baker et al 2003 and Reid 2006) nor the Colorado chipmunk (*N. quadrivittatus*), as presently defined, occurs anywhere near Walnut Canyon NM. The Hopi chipmunk occurs primarily in eastern Utah, edging into extreme northeastern Arizona in the Monument Valley/Page area, and the Colorado chipmunk occurs in Colorado and New Mexico, extending into northeastern Arizona in the area of Lukachukai south to Window Rock (see Reid 2006 for current maps of the ranges of all three of these species).

We did not record gray-collared chipmunk during any of our field sampling, but we did not conduct surveys specifically for diurnal small mammals. For the period 1936 – 1975, there are a total of 58 NPS natural history observation cards for gray-collared chipmunk, with comments including "common" and "very common." The cards list these chipmunks as being seen in every month of the year at Walnut Canyon. There are three museum specimens of gray-collared chipmunk from the monument, including two collected by Milton Wetherill, labeled "Walnut Canyon Nat'l Mon., San Francisco Mts." (MNA, 10/30/1938)

Cliff chipmunk (*Neotamias dorsalis*) – See the discussion under gray-collared chipmunk regarding the genus name used for the chipmunks in the western U.S.) Although we did not conduct extensive surveys for diurnal small mammals at Walnut Canyon, the aggregate of records that we compiled indicates that cliff chipmunks are the less common of the two chipmunk species at the monument. We recorded two individuals of this species, one in pinyon – juniper along the

south rim of the canyon just east of Cherry Canyon on 17 August 2003, and another in the canyon bottom 50 m east of Santa Fe Dam on 9 September 2004. There are three entries for cliff chipmunk in the NPS natural history observation cards, in pinyon / juniper habitat in the vicinity of the visitor center, in 1971, 1972, and 1974 (by way of comparison, there are 58 cards for gray-collared chipmunk; see above). This may simply reflect the relative abundance of the two species in the area where most of the observation card data are collected, or it may be a fair reflection of which of the two species is more numerous. There are four specimens of cliff chipmunk from Walnut Canyon, all housed at MNA. There is also a museum specimen from "5 mi E & 0.5 mi S of Flagstaff" (NAU, 14 October 1967), which would be within a couple of km of the west end of Walnut Canyon NM. There is one other specimen from "Walnut" (USNM, date unavailable), which is about 5 km (3 miles) east of the east end of the new addition of Walnut Canyon NM.

Abert's squirrel (*Sciurus aberti*) – Abert's squirrel is common in the ponderosa forests at Walnut Canyon. We only conducted incidental surveys for diurnal small mammals, and the only Abert's squirrel that we recorded in our survey database was an individual in ponderosa forest on the canyon rim near the Arizona Trail on 10 September 2004. NPS natural history observation card records variously describe the species as "common" to "abundant" to "seen occasionally in winter." The Museum of Northern Arizona has four specimens from Walnut Canyon, and there is also a specimen of Abert's squirrel from "1 mi NW Walnut Canyon Nat. Mon. Hdqts." at the University of Illinois Museum.

Golden-mantled ground squirrel (*Spermophilus lateralis*) – The golden-mantled ground squirrel was formerly included in the genus *Citellus*. NPS natural history observation card records include a single report in 1936. Subsequent cards describe the species as "common." This species frequently becomes relatively tame in visitor areas of National Parks and similar areas. The Museum of Northern Arizona has a total of five specimens from "Walnut Canyon Nat'l Mon." (11/19/1936) and from "Walnut Canyon Nat'l Mon., San Francisco Mts." (10/30/1938). Three of these are labeled as "*Citellus lateralis.*"

Rock squirrel (*Spermophilus variegatus*) – The rock squirrel was formerly called *Citellus variegatus*. Rock squirrels are fairly common at Walnut Canyon NM. We recorded one individual with an automatic infrared camera setup in the canyon bottom about 750 m west of Santa Fe Dam on 1 October 2004. The camera was set up overlooking an area of extensive burrowing under and around a tree in the canyon bottom. NPS natural history observation cards have single observations of rock squirrels, and other cards note them as "common." One card notes a rock squirrel gathering and eating pinyon nuts. The Museum of Northern Arizona has two specimens of rock squirrel collected from Walnut Canyon.

## Family Geomyidae – Pocket gophers

Botta's pocket gopher (*Thomomys bottae*) – Botta's pocket gopher was formerly included under the name *Thomomys fulvus* in this area, and some older NPS reports for Walnut Canyon used this name. Traps for pocket gophers are generally kill traps, and we did not use any such traps during our sampling. NPS natural history observation card records include comments such as "common throughout the yellow pine belt," "very plentiful," and "spreading." The nearest museum specimen to Walnut Canyon that we found was from "East Flagstaff" (NAU, 28 April 1978).

## Family Muridae – Mice, rats, and voles

Mogollon vole (*Microtus mogollonensis*) – This species is related to the southerly-distributed Mexican vole (*M. mexicanus*), and until recently it was considered a subspecies of that taxon (and still is by some authors – see Reid 2006). This species has also been considered part of a different subspecies, the Navajo vole (*M. mexicanus navaho*; see Hoffmeister 1986). We caught a single Mogollon vole in grassland in the canyon bottom next to the Santa Fe Dam on 28 September 2004. There are also two NPS natural history observation cards that note single voles seen in 1972 at the visitor center, and in 1974 along the Island Trail. In our initial museum searches, the nearest specimen of Mogollon vole that we could find was "3 mi N of Walnut Canyon Nat'l Mon." (NAU, 03/24/1965). However, we subsequently found two specimens at MNA that were collected from Walnut Canyon NM, but were evidently uncataloged at the time of our first search.

Arizona woodrat (*Neotoma devia*) – Earlier references (e.g. Hoffmeister, 1986), Burt and Grossenheider, 1980) listed this form as the desert woodrat, *N. lepida*. The "desert woodrats" south and east of the Colorado River are now recognized as a separate species, *N. devia*, which is given the common name 'Arizona woodrat.' The Arizona woodrat is at least fairly common at Walnut Canyon. We captured three individuals at three sites: one at the old ranger cabin on 18 August 2003, one in the canyon bottom west of Cherry Canyon on 1 September 2003, and one along the west side of the canyon in the new western addition to the monument on 12 September 2003.

Mexican woodrat (*Neotoma mexicana*) – Mexican woodrats are present at Walnut Canyon in at least small numbers. We caught a single individual in the canyon bottom in the northeast part of the monument on 20 October 2004. There are two museum specimens of Mexican woodrat from Walnut Canyon (both at MNA), including "Walnut Canyon Ranger Station, Walnut Canyon Nat'l Mon." (MNA, 11/01/1936). NPS natural history observation cards for woodrats just say 'woodrat' without noting particular species.

Stephens's woodrat (*Neotoma stephensi*) – Stephens's woodrat is fairly common at Walnut Canyon NM. We caught a total of four (the most of any of the small numbers of woodrats that we caught) at the following locations: canyon bottom west of the Island Trail (random point # 752) on 27 August 2002, one along the edge of the north side of the canyon on 7 September 2002, one in the canyon bottom W of Cherry Canyon on 1 September 2003, and one in the canyon bottom in the northeast end of the monument on 20 October 2004. There is one specimen of Stephens's woodrat from Walnut Canyon, housed at the Museum of Northern Arizona. There is also a specimen from "Walnut Canyon, 5 mi. S Mt. Elden, 6500 ft" at the University of Illinois Museum (date not available). A specimen from "5 mi SE of Flagstaff" (NAU, 08/25/1967) would also have been collected relatively close to Walnut Canyon NM.

Northern grasshopper mouse (*Onychomys leucogaster*) – The northern grasshopper mouse is uncommon to rare at Walnut Canyon. We trapped a single individual in the canyon bottom in the northeast end of the monument on 20 October 2004. The nearest museum specimen (USNM) is from "Walnut" (= Winona), about 5 km (3 miles) east of Walnut Canyon.

Brush mouse (*Peromyscus boylii*) – The brush mouse is one of three species of Peromyscus that were about equally common in our trap captures. We found brush mice to be widely distributed throughout the monument, from the canyon rims to the canyon bottom, and in areas of ponderosa pine forest, pinyon-juniper, and even one individual captured in grassland near the northeast boundary of the monument. There are seven specimens of brush mouse from Walnut Canyon NM. Three of these are at the Museum of Northern Arizona, and four are from "5 mi S Mt. Elden, Walnut Canyon, 6500 ft;" (USNM, no date). Two other specimens (both at the Northern Arizona University museum) are nearby: "6 mi E of Flagstaff" (10/14/1967); and "12 mi E of Flagstaff."

Deer mouse (*Peromyscus maniculatus*) – Deer mice were the most numerous small mammal in our trap captures at Walnut Canyon, with just slightly higher numbers than either pinyon mice or brush mice. We also found them widely distributed throughout the monument, and in virtually all habitats sampled, from grassland through ponderosa pine forest. The Museum of Northern Arizona has a total of seven specimens of deer mouse from "Walnut Canyon Nat'l Mon." Six of these were collected in January and February, 1937

Pinyon mouse (*Peromyscus truei*) – Pinyon mice are common at Walnut Canyon, and we caught them in only slightly lower numbers than deer mice. They were more limited in their distribution than either brush mice or deer mice, however. We caught them primarily in the eastern half of the monument and in the woods along the entrance road, and primarily in pinyon – juniper (19 captures were in habitat categorized as pinyon – juniper, two were in ponderosa woodland, two were in grassland, and two were in "canyon bottom" habitat). There are two specimens of pinyon mouse collected from Walnut Canyon NM (both housed at MNA). There are also specimens from just west and just east of the monument: "6 mi E of Flagstaff" (NAU Museum, 10/14/1967); and "12 mi E of Flagstaff" (NAU Museum, 05/20/1967).

Western harvest mouse (*Reithrodontomys megalotis*) – Western harvest mice appear to be relatively rare at Walnut Canyon NM, though they are frequently thought to be under-represented in trap captures relative to their abundance. We caught three harvest mice during our sampling, the first records of this species at Walnut Canyon. One was along the road on the northern edge of the monument, at the edge of ponderosa pine forest on 18 September 2004, and the other two were in grassland along the canyon rim at the northeast end of the monument on 18 October 2004. We found no museum specimens very close to Walnut Canyon. The nearest specimens of western harvest mouse were "Canyon Padre, 20 mi E of Flagstaff" and "Canyon Padre, 1 mi W of I-40 bridge, 22 mi E of Flagstaff" (both MNA, 08/05/1971). These locations are approximately 13 – 14 km (8 – 9 miles) east of Walnut Canyon.

### Family Erethizontidae – New World porcupines

North American porcupine (*Erethizon dorsatum*) – Porcupines are fairly common at Walnut Canyon, though we did not record any sightings during fieldwork for this study. Porcupine numbers have evidently been high enough previously that the Park Service instituted a control program in 1962 because of tree damage (NPS natural history observation card). Perhaps not surprisingly, porcupines are poorly represented in museum collections in this region. The nearest record we found to Walnut Canyon was "Mt. Dell Road (S of Flagstaff Airport)" (NAU, 9 October 1969).

## Order Carnivora – Carnivores

### Family Canidae – Dogs, foxes, and wolves

Coyote (*Canis latrans*) – The coyote seems to be fairly common at Walnut Canyon, though we did not record any with infrared automatic cameras set at night, nor did we have any incidental sightings during our surveys. There are 70 NPS natural history observation card records of this species between 1937 and 1975. Some so these notes suggest that coyote numbers were low during the 1950's in the Walnut Canyon area. The nearest museum specimen of coyote that we found to Walnut Canyon was from "4.5 mi E of Flagstaff, I-40" (NAU, 01/05/1975). This is 5 or 6 km from the monument.

Common gray fox (*Urocyon cinereoargenteus*) – We recorded what appeared to be two different gray foxes at the same site on the same night with an automatic camera placement in the bottom of Walnut Canyon 750 m west of Santa Fe Dam on 23 October 2004. This site is in a section of narrows in the main canyon. NPS observation card records include notes on an adult gray fox with four pups, on 20 June 1970, and a gray fox with a dead rock squirrel, also in June 1970. The nearest museum record that we found for gray fox to Walnut Canyon is from Anderson Canyon on Anderson Mesa (U.S. National Museum, cited in Hoffmeister 1986).

### Family Ursidae – Bears

American black bear (*Ursus americanus*) – A single black bear was recorded during the period of our surveys with an infrared automatic camera. This camera placement was set up by Brandon Holton by a pool in the bottom of Cherry Canyon pools on 1 September 2004. In the period between 1938 and 2000, there were 13 NPS natural history observation card records of black bears at Walnut Canyon. These records included sign, such as tracks. The most recent record we found was of a large adult on the road at night, just north of the Arizona Trail, on 16 June 2000.

### Family Procyonidae – Raccoons, ringtails, and coatis

Ringtail (*Bassariscus astutus*) – The ringtail is probably fairly common at Walnut Canyon. We did not record this ringtails during our surveys, and the only confirmed record that we have from within the monument is an NPS natural history observation card record of a ringtail in the canyon below the first Rim Trail overlook (1972, Michael Salomonson). However, this is not surprising, given the strictly nocturnal and secretive nature of this species. Ringtails typically live among cliffs and boulder areas, and they probably occur primarily below the canyon rim at Walnut Canyon, where few people go (especially at night). The nearest museum specimen of ringtail to Walnut Canyon is a road-killed individual from east Route 66 at Fanning Drive (NAU, 6 June 2007). Otherwise, the nearest specimens are from Oak Creek Canyon.

White-nosed coati (*Nasua narica*) – Some sources use the scientific name *Nasua nasua* for this species, and the common name coatimundi, or "chulo". The coati is known from Walnut Canyon and the surrounding area from observations and at least one specimen from the period 1952 – 1958. Specific records, from NPS natural history observation cards, include two that were seen just outside monument on 19 August 1952 by Meredith Guillet, who was superintendent of the monument at that time; and one observed on the monument entrance road by Regional Archaeologist Charlie Steen in June 1958. This latter record is the last report that we found for coati in the area. There appeared to be a large die-off of coatis in 1960 – 61 (Hoffmeister 1986, Kaufmann et al. 1976), a couple of years after this. There is no evidence now of a persistent population of coatis anywhere nearby, and we list the species as historic/extirpated from Walnut Canyon NM.

Kaufmann et al. (1976), with little justification, dismissed all records of coati outside of the southeastern corner of Arizona as escaped captives. This is in spite of numerous records ranging from the Salt River and Verde Valley to the area of Prescott, Walnut Canyon, and Anderson Mesa, the presence of multiple animals and documented persistence over several years in some areas, and the fact that many of these records are from the 1950's, during a time when coatis were evidently numerous and seemed to be expanding their range. The evidence (including that in Kaufmann et al.) seems to point more strongly toward natural expansion over a period of decades, followed by decline in the northern parts of this range (see also Wallmo and Gallizioli 1954, and Wetherill 1957).

Northern raccoon (*Procyon lotor*) – Also called simply 'raccoon.' We did not record raccoons during our fieldwork for this project. However, they are reported from visitor center / housing area, and probably occur along the canyon bottom in Walnut Canyon as well. In nearby Flagstaff, they are fairly common in old residential neighborhoods. Given this, there are surprisingly few museum records from the area. The nearest specimen we could find to Walnut Canyon was "D.O.R. on Hwy 89A S of Flagstaff near Fry Canyon" (NAU, 18 September 1974; "D.O.R." = 'dead on road'). NPS natural history observation cards include reports around the residence area and observations of tracks in different areas.

## Family Mustelidae – Weasels, otters, and badgers

Long-tailed weasel (*Mustela frenata*) – The long-tailed weasel is at least a rare resident of Walnut Canyon. We did not record this species during our surveys, but there are three NPS natural history observation cards for weasels at Walnut Canyon: one at the visitor center porch in August 1971; one along the Island Trail in June 1972; and one crossing the road near the entrance station in July 1974. The nearest museum specimens are from "1.5 mi S Lower Lake Mary dam D.O.R" (NAU, 21 June 1981; "D.O.R." = 'dead on road') and from "D.O.R on Hwy 66, E of Flagstaff" (NAU, 9 April 1969).

American badger (*Taxidea taxus*) – We did not record badgers during our surveys at Walnut Canyon, and the closest museum specimen that we located is from "1.5 mi E of Winona" (MNA, 05/19/1985). This is about 7 km (4.5 miles) east of the east end of Walnut Canyon NM. Nonetheless, the species is evidently not uncommon in parts of Walnut Canyon NM. Between 1964 and 1969, there were 19 natural history observation card records of badgers in the monument, including records of burrows and digging.

## Family Mephitidae – Skunks

White-backed hog-nosed skunk (*Conepatus leuconotus*) – This species is also called hog-nosed skunk or western hog-nosed skunk, and some sources (e.g. Hoffmeister 1986) use the scientific name *C. mesoleucus*. The eastern hog-nosed skunk (split out as *C. leuconotus)* is sometimes treated as separate from the western hog-nosed skunk (*C. mesoleucus*), but Baker et al. (2003) and Reid (2006) treat the group as a single species. White-backed hog-nosed skunks appear to be fairly common at Walnut Canyon. We photographed one individual in the canyon bottom about 750 m west of Santa Fe Dam on 19 October 2004 with one of the infrared automatic camera traps. We also trapped a single juvenile in the residence area north of the visitor center. We did not find any NPS observation card records of this species, but that may simply reflect failure to distinguish this species from the superficially similar striped skunk. This species is occasionally seen in residential areas in Flagstaff, and there is a museum specimen from "Big Anderson Tank, approx. 7 mi S of I-40 on Buffalo Ranch Road" (NAU, 8 August 1975; this location is along Anderson Canyon, on Anderson Mesa).

Striped skunk (*Mephitis mephitis*) – Striped skunks are common at Walnut Canyon. We photographed two with infrared automatic camera sets, including one at an area of intensive burrowing about 750 m west of Santa Fe Dam on 1 October 2004, and one in the canyon bottom near the confluence of Cherry Canyon and the main part of Walnut Canyon on 19 October 2004, along a well-developed game trail. NPS natural history observation card records have descriptive notes on striped skunks ranging from "common" to "seen occasionally." As noted above, it is possible that some of these records may be confused with the white-backed hog-nosed skunk.

### Family Felidae – Cats

Bobcat (*Lynx rufus*) – Called *Felis rufus* by older references. Bobcats appear to be fairly common at Walnut Canyon. We photographed two with infrared automatic camera placements. These included one in the canyon bottom about 250 m east of Santa Fe Dam on the evening of 29 September 2004, and one in the canyon bottom 750 m west of Santa Fe Dam on 18 October 2004. Between 1950 and 1980, NPS natural history observation card records housed at the Flagstaff Area

Monuments headquarters included a total of 57 entries for bobcat, including sign. The nearest museum record is from "1 mi S of Winona" (NAU, 19 November 1970).

Mountain lion (*Puma concolor*) – Older sources use the scientific name *Felis concolor*. There are many different common names for this wide-ranging species, with the most common alternative names in our area being cougar and puma. Mountain lions are common residents of Walnut Canyon, but are rarely seen. There are records from NPS natural history observation cards of mountain lions in all months of the year. Some cards have noted sightings in some of the archaeological dwelling sites, and have also reported hunter kills of lions in the Walnut Canyon area.

## Order Artiodactyla – Even-toed Ungulates

### Family Tayassuidae – Peccaries

Collared peccary (*Pecari tajacu*) – Some references use the scientific name *Tayassu tajacu*, and one NPS observation card uses the old name *Pecari angulatus*. 'Javelina' is widely used in the Southwest as the common name for this species. The collared peccary is a recent arrival to the area of Walnut Canyon (see below), having expanded its range from southern Arizona. It is now fairly common in and around the monument, and ranges from the canyon bottom through the fields of the adjacent uplands (Charles van Riper, USGS Southwest Biological Science Center, pers. comm.). We photographed one individual with an automatic infrared camera set in the canyon bottom 250 m E of Santa Fe Dam on 29 September 2004. We also observed small herds of peccaries on two other occasions: a group of 5 in the canyon bottom 2 km east of Santa Fe Dam on 9 September 2004; and 3 individuals foraging near garbage cans in the open ponderosa pine forest of the NPS residence area on 19 October 2004. The collared peccary was first reported (on an NPS natural history observation card) on November 1954. The full text of this entry reads: "On the evening of November 9, while investigating strange noises which were thought to be the grunts and gasping breath of perhaps a wounded buck, the Superintendent inadvertently found himself right in the center of a herd of Javelina. This is the first recorded sighting of these animals at Walnut Canyon." A female with two half-grown young was noted in a sighting on 28 January 1955. Additional sightings followed in 1956 and 1957, and they have been recorded on scattered occasions at Walnut Canyon since that time. Peccaries are now known to have spread farther north, to the south rim of Grand Canyon.

### Family Cervidae – Deer

Elk (*Cervus canadensis*) – Some references use the scientific name *C. elaphus*, and the common name "Wapiti" is used in parts of the range. All of the elk in Arizona are descended from animals introduced from the Rocky Mountains. The native elk in Arizona ("Merriam's elk") is now extinct, and was not known to occur anywhere near Walnut Canyon. Hence, we list elk in this area as "non-native." Elk are fairly common in and around Walnut Canyon. We did not specifically survey for large mammals, but we did encounter elk during the course of other fieldwork. Our observations include a single individual west of Santa Fe Dam, flushed from the canyon bottom on 9 September 2004, and a group of six individuals of mixed age / sex (adult females with juveniles) 100 m west of the visitor center in ponderosa pine forest on 18 October 2004. One observation card record may mark the earliest recorded sighting of elk in the area of Walnut Canyon. The card notes that in May 1937 "an elk was seen ~ 1 ½ mi. W of the Monument." The sighting was noteworthy enough that it was included in the "NPS Monthly Report" of the time. This is the earliest record we could find for elk in this area.

Mule deer (*Odocoileus hemionus*) – Mule deer are common at Walnut Canyon. We did not specifically conduct surveys for large mammals, but we did record one mule deer with one of our infrared automatic cameras set along a game trail in the canyon bottom near the confluence of Cherry Canyon with the main part of Walnut Canyon, on 19 October 2004. Numerous NPS natural history observation cards report mule deer in all months of the year at Walnut Canyon, and herds of up to 10–14 in fall and winter. Fawns have been reported in July and later.

### Family Antilocapridae – Pronghorn

Pronghorn (*Antilocapra americana*) – Pronghorn are fairly common transients through Walnut Canyon, particularly in the eastern part of the monument. There are a few places in the east / northeast extension of the monument where pronghorn habitually cross the canyon, moving to and from the open areas on the north side, to areas south and east, towards Anderson Mesa (Charles van Riper, USGS Southwest Biological Science Center, pers. comm.). Distribution of

pronghorn has probably become more restricted in the area around the monument and numbers may have declined somewhat in the last half century. NPS natural history observation card records dating back to 1936 report pronghorn to the west, north, east, and south of the monument. Encroaching development from the west now probably largely excludes them from this area. Numbers recorded on natural history observation cards range up to 24 ("watering at (Smith's) tank...," July 1936) to 30 (herd seen along the monument entrance road, November 1963). Numbers seen in the area now are in the range of 12 – 14 individuals (C. van Riper, pers. comm.). There is one museum specimen from "N of Walnut Canyon Ranger Station" (MNA, 02/28/1940).

### Family Bovidae – Cattle, antelope, sheep, and goats

Domestic cattle (*Bos taurus*) – Up until recently, occasional trespass animals made their way onto the monument. They may continue to show up in areas with fence breaks.

Bighorn sheep (*Ovis canadensis*) – Historic occurrence – Bighorn formerly occurred in this area, but have long since been extirpated. The Museum of Northern Arizona has a specimen of bighorn from "Walnut Canyon Nat'l Mon.," dated 1 November 1936, and there is also a specimen from Mount Elden, about 8 km (5 mi.) north of Walnut Canyon (U.S. National Museum). The subspecies that formerly occurred in the area of Sunset Crater was the desert bighorn, (*O. canadensis mexicana* or *O. canadensis nelsoni*, depending on the author – e.g. Hoffmeister 1986, McCutchen 1995).

## Other potential species at Walnut Canyon:

Crawford's desert shrew (*Notiosorex crawfordi*) – Crawford's desert shrew is probably present in some of the habitats at Walnut Canyon. Until fairly recently there were very few records of desert shrews from Arizona, but surveys targeting this species have turned them up in a wide range of habitats, from desert scrub to pinyon-juniper and ponderosa woodland (Hoffmeister 1986). There are many records from the area of Wupatki NM (see Appendix 4) and a single specimen has been recorded from one mile north of Sunset Crater (Hoffmeister 1986), so they are known to occur in habitats present at Walnut Canyon. Sampling methods specifically targeting shrews will likely prove desert shrew to be part of the Walnut Canyon mammal fauna.

Merriam's shrew (*Sorex merriami*) – We did not record Merriam's shrew nor any other shrew species at Walnut Canyon, but our sampling methods were not effective for shrews. The nearest museum specimen records we found for Merriam's shrew were from "13 mi NNE of Flagstaff" (NAU,12/08/1969), 2 specimens from "Flagstaff" (both NAU – 10/22/1970, 09/08/1975), "Flagstaff, Mars Hill" (NAU,11/16/1971), and "San Francisco peaks, inner basin" (NAU,07/02/1971) Hoffmeister (1986) describes habitat for this species as "cool grassy places...near coniferous forests," and Armstrong and Jones (1971) note that Merriam's shrew occurs in drier habitats than other Sorex species, including pine – Douglas fir – aspen woodlands. Shrews are notoriously under-represented in most mammal surveys (including our work) and we think it is likely that Merriam's shrew occurs at Walnut Canyon.

Townsend's big-eared bat (*Corynorhinus townsendii*) – Called *Plecotus townsendii* by some references. We did not encounter Townsend's big-eared bat in the course of our surveys, and the species has not been recorded from the monument previously. The nearest museum specimen we could find was from "Oak Creek Canyon, Pumphouse Wash" (NAU, 30 May 1968). The species is also fairly common at Wupatki NM. Although the Kaibab Limestone forms the upper layer of the cliffs at Walnut Canyon, we do not know of any large, high caves within the monument boundaries of the sort that are used by Townsend's big-eared bat for maternity colonies. It is possible, however, that single big-eared bats may occur at Walnut Canyon, either on a regular basis or as occasional visitors. At other archaeological monuments, such as Montezuma Castle NM in central Arizona, Townsend's big-eared bats are known to roost in the dark recesses in the back of cliff dwellings.

Western red bat (*Lasiurus blossevillii*) – In older references, the eastern and western red bats are treated as a single species (the red bat, *L. borealis*). The two species are now recognized as distinct (though they are difficult to distinguish, even in the hand), with only the western red bat likely to be found in Arizona. Records of western red bat in Arizona are few and widely scattered, with the nearest record to Walnut Canyon being at "mouth Bright Angel Creek, N Side GCNP (Grand Canyon National Park)" (University of Illinois specimen, cited in Hoffmeister 1986). This species is migratory, and could occur at Walnut Canyon as a rare resident, or during spring or fall migrations to and from areas farther north. The dearth of records may reflect in part the difficulty of detecting nocturnal bats during their limited migration passages through the state.

Western pipistrelle (*Pipistrellus hesperus*) – We did not capture nor record calls of western pipistrelles in or near Walnut Canyon, and the species has not been documented from the area in the past. This is somewhat surprising, as the canyon walls of Walnut Canyon provide the typical habitat associated with this diminutive bat. In Arizona, however, most records of pipistrelles are from lower elevations (Hoffmeister 1986). The nearest museum specimen to Walnut Canyon was collected at "Rio de Flag, MNA grounds, 3 mi N of Flagstaff" (MNA, 13 September 1972)

Long-legged myotis (*Myotis volans*) – We did not record this species, either as a mist-net capture or with Anabat, and it has not been recorded previously at Walnut Canyon. Nonetheless, we expect it is probably present, as a rare resident or occasional visitor. It has been recorded nearby in similar habitat, at the "Continental Country Club, Flagstaff" (MNA, 30 May 1976). There are also museum specimens from "SW base of Mt. Elden, Flagstaff" (NAU, 23 June 1968). The long-legged myotis is associated with ponderosa pine and other coniferous forest habitat (Hoffmeister 1986) so the species is probably found somewhere at Walnut Canyon NM, though it appears that it is not common.

Gunnison's prairie dog (*Cynomys gunnisoni*) – We did not record Gunnison's prairie dog during our sampling at Walnut Canyon, though we did not spend much time surveying for diurnal small mammals. This species occurs in open fields, grasslands, and along road edges to the west, north, and east of the monument, however, and it would be surprising if it did not occur at least as an occasional visitor to Walnut Canyon, especially in the eastern extension of the monument. In spite of its abundance, there are surprisingly few museum records of this prairie dog in the vicinity of Walnut Canyon. The nearest specimen that we could find was "ca. 5 mi S of Flagstaff on Lake Mary Rd." (MNA, 1 April 1932).

White-tailed antelope squirrel (*Ammospermophilus leucurus*) – The name *Citellus leucurus* is used by some older references and museum specimen labels. We did not trap nor observe white-tailed antelope squirrels during our surveys at Walnut Canyon, and there are no previous records for this species from the monument. The nearest museum specimen is, however, from similar habitat in "Canyon Padre, 22 mi E of Flagstaff" (MNA,04/05/1972). This is approximately 14 km (9 miles) east of Walnut Canyon. This species may be present within monument boundaries, and is to be looked for in the lower elevation, more arid parts of the eastern end of the monument.

Spotted ground squirrel (*Spermophilus spilosoma*) – The U.S. National Museum has two specimens from "Walnut" and "Walnut 5 mi from Turkey Tanks." "Walnut" is an old name for Winona, and is about 5 km (3 miles) east of the east end of Walnut Canyon NM. This species primarily occurs in grassland habitats, is regionally rare, and is probably not present at Walnut Canyon.

Ord's kangaroo rat (*Dipodomys ordii*) – We did not encounter kangaroo rats in any of our trapping at Walnut Canyon, and did not see evidence, such as burrows, of their presence. There is an NPS natural history observation card of two kangaroo rats seen at the 'Old Ranger Cabin' in August 1955, however this site in mature ponderosa forest is not at all typical habitat for this species. Salomonson (1973) listed Ord's kangaroo rat as present at Walnut Canyon but provided no documentation, other than saying the species "(has) been seen in the past." Perhaps this is in reference to the questionable observation card discussed above. The closest occurrence that we found for Ord's kangaroo rat to Walnut Canyon was "3 mi NW Winona, 6400 ft, 6500 ft" (U.S. National Museum, cited in Hoffmeister 1986).

Silky pocket mouse (*Perognathus flavus*) – We did not capture any pocket mice during our surveys, and none have been taken from within the boundaries of Walnut Canyon NM in the past. Salomonson (1973) listed this species as hypothetical at the monument, but it has been included in subsequent checklists. The nearest museum specimen locations that we found were "Winona, 6400 ft" (8 specimens, Museum of Vertebrate Zoology, Berkeley; cited in Hoffmeister 1986) and "Walnut" (= Winona; 1 specimen, U.S. National Museum, cited in Hoffmeister 1986). Winona / Walnut is approximately 5 km (3 mi.) east of the east end of the new eastern addition to Walnut Canyon. This species occurs in arid grasslands and "sagebrush-cactus association" (Hoffmeister 1986) and small numbers may be present in suitable pockets of habitat in the eastern extension of Walnut Canyon NM.

Plains pocket mouse (*Perognathus flavescens*) This species is called the Apache pocket mouse (*P. apache*) by Hoffmeister (1986), but recent sources do not recognize *P. apache* as being distinct from the plains pocket mouse (*P. flavescens*). There are two specimens from about 5 km (3 mi.) east of the east end of the eastern addition to Walnut Canyon: "Winona, 6400 ft" (MVZ, no date); and "Walnut, 5 mi from Turkey Tanks" (USNM, no date; as noted, "Walnut" is an old name for Winona). Another specimen from "3 mi NW Winona, 6400-6500 ft." (USNM, no date) is also nearby, and is at the same elevation as Walnut Canyon. Hoffmeister (1986) notes that this species seems to be strongly associated with sandy soils and shifting sands (including lava sand). He further notes that "near Winona they

[plains pocket mice] were taken among scattered yellow pines in lava sands, sagebrush, rabbitbrush, and juniper." If there are similar habitats with sandy substrate in the eastern end of Walnut Canyon NM, it would not be surprising to ind the plains pocket mouse there.

Western white-throated woodrat (*Neotoma albigula*) – This species is also called simply "white-throated woodrat." However, recent genetic studies have led to the recognition of the white-throated woodrats east of the Rio Grande as a separate species (the eastern white-throated woodrat, *N. leucodon*). Hence, western white-throated woodrat is the preferred common name. This species has not been reported previously at Walnut Canyon, and we could not confirm its presence either, but suspect it may occur in the lower elevations of the monument. A juvenile woodrat caught near random point 735 at the north end of the entrance road on 14 August 2002 was thought to be this species, but the identification could not be confirmed.

White-footed mouse (*Peromyscus leucopus*) – The white-footed mouse is very similar in appearance to the deer mouse, and is probably often overlooked in Arizona (Hoffmeister 1986). We did not record white-footed mice in our trapping at Walnut Canyon. The nearest museum record is from Turkey Tanks, about 9 km (5.5 mi.) from the east end of Walnut Canyon NM. Turkey Tanks is connected to Walnut Canyon via San Francisco Wash and Walnut Creek, so it is possible that white-footed mice will eventually be found within the monument boundaries. Hoffmeister (1986) notes that white-footed mice in northern and central Arizona have been found in dense grass and weeds and clumps of tamarisk along streams and other damp areas, so this species should be looked for in open canyon bottom areas at Walnut Canyon.

Western spotted skunk (*Spilogale gracilis*) – Taxonomists have gone back and forth between recognizing one, wide-ranging 'spotted skunk' (*S. putorius*) in North America, and splitting this group up. Several lines of evidence point to there being more than one distinct form, and most references now consider *S. gracilis* to be a different species from the eastern spotted skunk, *S. putorius*. Western spotted skunks are almost certainly present and fairly common at Walnut Canyon. However, they can be quite secretive and difficult to detect. We did not observe them during our surveys, and did not record them with infrared cameras for nocturnal species. There are no museum specimen records from near Walnut Canyon (the nearest record that we know of is a road-killed individual found near the east entrance to Sunset Crater – see Appendix 5). There is only a single NPS natural history observation card record of a skunk that 'might have been a spotted skunk.' Nonetheless, Walnut Canyon provides suitable habitat for spotted skunks, and we expect that specific surveys for this species will eventually find it at this location.

# Appendix 4

## Annotated mammal species list for Wupatki National Monument, Arizona.

Information provided for each species includes presence or absence within the Monument, documentation (e.g. museum specimens, trap capture, or sightings), and what is known of the species' distribution and abundance. Museum abbreviations include: MNA – Museum of Northern Arizona; NAU – Northern Arizona University Vertebrate Museum; UI – University of Illinois Museum; and USNM – United States National Museum.

## Order Insectivora – Insectivores

### Family Soricidae – Shrews

Crawford's desert shrew (*Notiosorex crawfordi*) – This species is also called simply 'desert shrew' (e.g. Hoffmeister 1986). There has been little trapping specifically targeting shrews at Wupatki, but the desert shrew appears to be relatively common and widespread in the area. Specimens have been collected at sites ranging from the west end of the monument (six specimens from the area of the Wupatki Road, approximately 1 mile east of U.S. Highway 89) to the Monument Headquarters area. A specimen from Hulls Canyon may have been collected within the monument, but the location was not stated precisely. It is at least close to the southern boundary of Wupatki. Habitats in these areas range from arid grassland to juniper savanna to cold desert scrub.

## Order Chiroptera – Bats

### Family Vespertilionidae – Vesper bats

Pallid bat (*Antrozous pallidus*) – Eight museum specimens from Wupatki were all taken from the area of the Monument headquarters and Heiser Spring, in the southern part of the Wupatki Basin. We did not capture nor record pallid bats at any of our sampling sites at Wupatki, suggesting that this species is relatively uncommon or local in its distribution at Wupatki. There is little or no surface water at Heiser Spring anymore, perhaps accounting for the lack of recent records of pallid bats in that area.

Townsend's big-eared bat (*Corynorhinus townsendii*) – Called *Plecotus townsendii* by some references. Townsend's big-eared bat is a year-round resident at Wupatki that is known to roost in several of the earth crack caves within the monument boundaries. We recorded this species at Arrowhead Tank and Doney Fissure in May (Persons and Drost 2001), and museum specimens have been collected from the monument headquarters area, Heiser Spring, and the Antelope Wash road. The Cave Research Foundation (1976) recorded Townsend's big-eared bats at four earth crack features, and indicated that some of these were hibernating. Likewise, Bain (1986) recorded hibernating big-eared bats at several earth crack caves during his winter surveys. Persons (2001) recorded one road-killed Townsend's big-eared bat, in grassland west of Lomaki (near mile post 2) in his study of road mortality at Wupatki.

Big brown bat (*Eptesicus fuscus*) – We did not record big brown bats from Wupatki, and there are no museum records nor other reports from within the monument boundaries. However, we did find big brown bats to be fairly common at Sunset Crater, and also recorded one at Rimmy Jim Tank near Gray Mountain, north of Wupatki. Based on these records, we expect the species is present on at least an occasional basis at Wupatki. If so, the lack of records from all sources indicates it is rare there.

Spotted bat (*Euderma maculatum*) – On May 11, 2000, we recorded the distinctive audible calls of one or more spotted bats at the Black Falls crossing of the Little Colorado River, along the eastern edge of Wupatki. Spotted bats were heard on at least two occasions that evening, flying over the river. Spotted bats fly long distances at night (40 km or more, straight-line distance), so we do not know whether the individuals heard were transients, or if they use the monument regularly. We do not know of any other records of spotted bat in the vicinity, but this species remains relatively poorly known and difficult to survey for.

Silver-haired bat (*Lasionycteris noctivagans*) – The silver-haired bat is known from Wupatki from a single specimen collected at Heiser Spring (University of Arizona collection). We did not record this species anywhere near Wupatki, and we know of no other nearby records. Silver-haired bat is typically a forest species, and is probably a rare visitor to Wupatki.

Hoary bat (*Lasiurus cinereus*) – Bateman (1981) caught a hoary bat at the sewage ponds near the Wupatki NM headquarters and visitor center. We recorded calls of a hoary bat along a driving transect through Sunset Crater NM on the evening of May 9, 2000. This is a highly migratory species of bat and its occurrence at Wupatki is probably limited to brief appearances as individual bats pass through during spring and fall migration.

California myotis (*Myotis californicus*) – The California myotis is a fairly common resident at Wupatki. We recorded it from May through October, at sites ranging from Citadel Sink to Arrowhead Tank to the Black Falls crossing. Museum specimens from Wupatki were taken from Heiser Spring and from along the Antelope Wash road. California myotis was the second most numerous bat that we recorded at Wupatki, and this is probably an accurate reflection of its abundance in the area.

Western small-footed myotis (*Myotis ciliolabrum*) – This species is sometimes treated under the name *M. leibii* (e.g. Hoffmeister 1986) and also *M. subulatus* (e.g. Burt and Grossenheider 1976). Formerly, it was thought that there was one 'small-footed myotis' that occurred across North America. It is now recognized that there are two species – an eastern form (*M. leibii*) and a western form (*M. ciliolabrum*). The western small-footed myotis is known from Wupatki on the basis of two specimens collected at Heiser Spring (University of Arizona Museum). We did not capture any small-footed myotis at Wupatki, but we did record calls and see flying bats that were probably this species at Doney Fissure (one, flying out of the fissure after nightfall) and Arrowhead Tank (several). Though there are other species with similar vocalizations, the character of the calls was most similar to *M. ciliolabrum*, and individuals that were seen flying had the fluttery, somewhat erratic flight of *M. ciliolabrum*. This species is evidently an uncommon resident or visitor to Wupatki.

Fringed myotis (*Myotis thysanodes*) – The fringed myotis was the most numerous bat that we recorded at Wupatki. It has been noted, by us and others, roosting in earth cracks and caves in and around Wupatki. Records from all sources extend from the Lomaki area to Arrowhead Tank, to Heiser Spring and the Black Falls crossing on the Little Colorado River.

Yuma myotis (*Myotis yumanensis*) – The Yuma myotis appears to be relatively rare at Wupatki, and this may reflect the scarcity of the open water habitat this species typically forages over and around. We recorded one or two individuals of Yuma myotis at the sewage ponds at the monument headquarters, and also at a small pool at the Black Falls crossing of the Little Colorado River. These are the first records of this species at Wupatki.

Western pipistrelle (*Pipistrellus hesperus*) – We recorded the calls of western pipistrelles at Citadel Sink. This is a cliff-roosting species, so Citadel Sink is one area of Wupatki where this species was to be expected. There are also several old museum records of western pipistrelle from Heiser Spring and the monument headquarters area. Western pipistrelles are 'early risers' and are often seen flying before it is fully dark.

### Family Molossidae – Free-tailed bats

Big free-tailed bat (*Nyctinomops macrotis*) – This species is called *Tadarida macrotis* in older references. We recorded calls of as many as five big free-tailed bats along the cliffs of Citadel Sink in October 2000. Big free-tailed bats roost in crevices in high cliffs, and it is likely that Citadel Sink harbors a roost site for this species. The calls of big free-tailed bat extend down into the human hearing range. The species also flies long distances while foraging, so big free-tails might reasonably be expected to be heard anywhere within the monument. This is the first record of big free-tailed bat at Wupatki.

Brazilian free-tailed bat (*Tadarida brasiliensis*) – This species is more commonly known as the Mexican free-tailed bat, but both Baker et al. (2003) and Reid (2006) have adopted the name 'Brazilian free-tailed bat.' We recorded calls of Brazilian free-tailed bats at the Black Falls crossing on the Little Colorado River during this study. There are no previous records of Brazilian free-tails at Wupatki or in the surrounding area. Lincoln (1961) predicted this species would be found at Wupatki, but it is evidently rare. Brazilian free-tail bats typically roost in large colonies in caves and similar sites, and there may be an absence of suitable roosting sites around Wupatki. There are no known roosts within the monument.

## Order Lagomorpha – Pikas, hares, and rabbits

### Family Leporidae – Hares and rabbits

Black-tailed jackrabbit (*Lepus californicus*) – We did not use field methods that specifically targeted lagomorphs, but recorded them during the course of other fieldwork (most often during night drives, and occasionally while walking to and from field sampling sites). Persons (2001) recorded black-tailed jackrabbits as one of the most numerous nocturnal mammals seen on the roads, second only to desert cottontail, and this agrees with our general observations during this study. Jackrabbits are seen in highest numbers in areas of juniper and juniper savanna.

Desert cottontail (*Sylvilagus audubonii*) – Desert cottontails are the most numerous medium-sized mammal at Wupatki, and are found across almost the entire monument. Persons (2001) found this to be the most numerous mammal species killed on the roads during his surveys in 1999 and 2000. Both from our general observations and from the data recorded by Persons, desert cottontails are most numerous in grassland habitats on the monument. They may be quite abundant in some years; we sometimes saw 30 – 40 or more cottontails along the roads in the evening or early morning.

## Order Rodentia – Rodents

### Family Sciuridae – Squirrels

White-tailed antelope squirrel (*Ammospermophilus leucurus*) – The name *Citellus leucurus* is used by some older references and museum specimen labels. Antelope squirrels (also called 'antelope ground squirrels') were the most numerous diurnal mammals seen during our surveys. They were also the most numerous diurnal mammal found dead on the road by Persons (2001) in his study of road mortality at Wupatki. We caught white-tailed antelope squirrels in desert scrub in the Wupatki Basin, at and to the south of Heiser Spring, and in Cedar Canyon.

Gunnison's prairie dog (*Cynomys gunnisoni*) – Gunnison's prairie dog is currently known in Wupatki only from the area east of the Lomaki Ruins. This species seems to have declined at Wupatki over the last 25 years. We observed single individuals in the vicinity of an old burrow complex east of the junction of the Lomaki road with the main park road, and in short grass east-northeast of Lomaki, near the north boundary fence. Persons (2001) recorded a road-killed prairie dog in the same area, at the junction of the main park road and the Lomaki road. Other locations of prairie dogs recorded on NPS observation cards between 1957 and 1984 include: 1) 1 mile south of Wupatki north entrance, 50 yards inside fence (along U.S. Highway 89; Township 25N, Range 8E, Section 10); 2) Township 25N, Range 8E, Section 2 (south of park entrance road, just east of milepost 1); 3) Township 25N, Range 8E, Section 14, northeast ¼ (northwest of Hulls Wash and southwest of West Mesa); 4) Township 25N, Range 9E, Section 4 – northwest ¼ of northwest ¼ of northwest ¼ (along south side of north boundary, about 2 km east of Lomaki); 5) Borrow pit, Township 25N, Range 10E, Section 12 (west of Little Colorado River, at east end of monument). A record from September 20, 1957 notes "First record of Prairie Dogs in this area... 8 or 10 holes are seemingly occupied but only one individual was seen." This record notes the location as "Big Hawk Valley," but no such map names could be found in or near Wupatki.

Cliff chipmunk (*Neotamias dorsalis*) – The western chipmunks have variously been placed in the genera *Tamias* and *Eutamias*. Recent taxonomic studies, including genetic analyses, point toward recognizing three different groups of chipmunks, with *Tamias* used for the eastern chipmunk, and *Neotamias* for all western U.S. chipmunks (Baker et al 2003; but also see Reid 2006, who uses *Tamias* for western chipmunks). Cliff Chipmunks are only known from a couple of records at Wupatki. The Museum of Northern Arizona has a specimen collected in August 1933 from Doney Mountain, and we observed a single individual on a low, rocky ridge along the south boundary fence west of Arrowhead Sink. We specifically searched for chipmunks in other areas along the south boundary, including Arrowhead Sink, Doney Mountain, and the Woodhouse Mesa area, but did not find them.

Spotted ground squirrel (*Spermophilus spilosoma*) – The spotted ground squirrel is rare at Wupatki. Specimens have been collected from the vicinity of the National Monument headquarters, and we observed a single individual northeast of Lomaki, near the north boundary of the monument. Hoffmeister (1986) notes that spotted ground squirrels occur over much the same range as Gunnison's prairie dogs, and the short grass / sparse vegetation habitat that they typically occur in (Streubel and Fitzgerald 1978) also is similar to that of prairie dogs. Hoffmeister (1986) also notes that these ground squirrels appear to have declined significantly in northern Arizona, possibly due to poisoning campaigns aimed at prairie dogs.

Rock squirrel (*Spermophilus variegatus*) – Rock squirrels are uncommon and local at Wupatki, probably reflecting the patchy distribution of the rock and boulder habitat that they are typically associated with. We trapped rock squirrels at Citadel Sink and at Lomaki, and Persons (2001) found one rock squirrel dead on the road between Lomaki and Citadel. We do not know of any previous specimen records from within the boundaries of Wupatki, but Hoffmeister (1986) plots a specimen location from Deadman Flat, south of Wupatki.

### Family Geomyidae – Pocket gophers

Botta's pocket gopher (*Thomomys bottae*) – Specimens at the Museum of Northern Arizona were labeled as *Thomomys fulvus*, which is now considered a subspecies of *T. bottae*. Pocket gophers spend the majority of their lives underground, but leave conspicuous evidence of their presence in the form of small mounds of loose dirt that they push up out of their burrows. Raised ridges marking the burrows themselves may also be seen. We did not use methods that target pocket gophers (primarily kill traps placed in burrows), but we did see pocket gopher sign in habitats ranging from the grasslands of Antelope Prairie to the desert scrub of Wupatki Basin. Specimens of Botta's pocket gopher – the only species that occurs in the region – have also been collected during previous studies (specimens at the Museum of Northern Arizona).

### Family Heteromyidae – Pocket mice and kangaroo rats

Rock pocket mouse (*Chaetodipus intermedius*) – Called *Perognathus intermedius* by some references, but separated out with the 'spiny' or 'coarse-furred' *Chaetodipus* pocket mice by recent authors. Rock pocket mice were one of the most numerous small mammals that we captured in our trapping at Wupatki; they were second in numbers only to Arizona pocket mice, both in overall captures and in our samples at randomly selected trapping sites. They seem to have been much less common in past collecting at the monument (total of eight specimens at MNA and NAU). This may reflect less trapping effort in the rock and boulder habitats that this species prefers. On the other hand, Trevor Persons (pers. comm.) noted that rock pocket mice were only present in numbers in one year during several consecutive years of trapping on his study site southeast of Wupatki. Hence, numbers of this species may simply vary widely from year to year.

Ord's kangaroo rat (*Dipodomys ordii*) – Ord's kangaroo rat appears to be uncommon and local at Wupatki. It is known from museum collections from Wupatki Basin ("Antelope Wash Road") and the vicinity of the monument headquarters and Heiser Spring. Persons (2001) noted a total of four road-killed kangaroo rats along the Wupatki Road between U.S. Highway 89 and Lomaki, and also found one near the south entrance, and one along the Wukoki Road. We did not capture any kangaroo rats, either in random sampling, or in targeted sampling (though we did not specifically target trapping for this species). Persons' fieldwork was conducted in 1999 and 2000, and the greater numbers he observed may reflect differences in year-to-year abundance, or perhaps a greater tendency for kangaroo rats to be killed on the road.

Arizona pocket mouse (*Perognathus amplus*) – The form occurring at Wupatki is the dark-pelaged 'Wupatki pocket mouse' (*P. amplus* subspecies *cineris*), which has a limited distribution from in and around Wupatki, north to the Echo Cliffs. The Wupatki pocket mouse was the most numerous nocturnal mammal in our trap sampling – both in random sampling and overall sampling. Most of our captures were from Great Basin Desert Scrub in the eastern part of the monument (Wupatki Basin). We also captured this species in the large canyons, such as Antelope Wash. Remarkably, Persons (2001) was able to identify many of the small mammals he found on the road in his study of road mortality at Wupatki. The two road-killed Wupatki pocket mice that he found were both between the monument headquarters and the south boundary. There are at least 10 specimens of this species collected at or near Wupatki.

Plains pocket mouse (*Perognathus flavescens*) – Some sources (e.g. Hoffmeister 1986) call the taxon in the Wupatki area the Apache pocket mouse (*P. apache*), separating out the populations in Utah, Arizona and western New Mexico from the wide-ranging *P. flavescens*. Recent sources lump the "Apache" pocket mouse with the plains pocket mouse, and we follow this arrangement. Plains pocket mice are uncommon and local at Wupatki. Museum specimens are from south of the monument headquarters and from near the Little Colorado River (indefinite location), and we captured individuals from Peshlaki Spring and the old NPS housing area near the monument's south boundary. This species is associated with sandy substrates (Hoffmeister 1986), which may limit its distribution at Wupatki.

Silky pocket mouse (*Perognathus flavus*) – Silky pocket mice are common at Wupatki in suitable habitat. This is the grassland pocket mouse at Wupatki, found at nearly all of our sampling sites from Antelope Prairie west. It also occurs in juniper savanna, in addition to more open grassland. All of our captures were from west of the Doney Cliffs, but silky pocket mice have also been recorded from scattered areas in the eastern half of the monument. There are museum specimen records from the Wupatki Pueblo and visitor center area, along the Antelope Wash road in Wupatki Basin, Heiser Spring, and near Wukoki.

### Family Muridae – Mice, rats, and voles

Western white-throated woodrat (*Neotoma albigula*) – This species is also called simply "white-throated woodrat," but recent genetic studies have led to the recognition of the white-throated woodrats east of the Rio Grande as a separate species (the eastern white-throated woodrat, *N. leucodon*). Hence, western white-throated woodrat is the preferred name. At Wupatki, this species is less numerous than either the Arizona woodrat or Stephens's woodrat. We found it at widely scattered locations from Peshlaki Spring and the base of Woodhouse Mesa, to the north slope of East Mesa, and the area of the prairie dog colony east of the Lomaki Road. An unusual occurrence of western white-throated woodrat was just east of U.S. 89 and south of the north entrance road, in grassland far from rocks, shrubs, or other typical habitat. This may have been a transient individual. Hoffmeister (1986) notes that this species is frequently associated with prickly pear and cholla cactus.

Arizona woodrat (*Neotoma devia*) – Earlier references (e.g. Hoffmeister, 1986), Burt and Grossenheider, 1980) listed this form as the desert woodrat, *N. lepida*. The "desert woodrats" south and east of the Colorado River are now recognized as a separate species, *N. devia*, which is given the common name 'Arizona woodrat.' This was the most numerous of the woodrat species that we captured during our sampling (among museum specimen collections, however, Stephens's woodrat is more numerous). Nearly all of our captures were associated with cliffs, mesa slopes, and canyons, mostly in the eastern half of the monument. Individuals were captured in Deadman Wash, Citadel Wash, Antelope Wash, and along the Doney Cliffs and Woodhouse Mesa. Individuals were also captured at the sewage ponds near the monument headquarters, and at Heiser Spring.

Stephens's woodrat (*Neotoma stephensi*) – Stephens's woodrat is common and widespread at Wupatki. We captured individuals at locations ranging from Cedar Canyon and Doney Fissure to the mouth of Antelope Wash, to Heiser Spring and the south entrance to the monument. Stephens's woodrat is frequently associated with juniper, and many of our captures were in juniper associations. We also recorded individuals from desert scrub, as at Heiser Spring. In the museum specimen records we reviewed, there were 23 Stephens's woodrats, compared to six Arizona woodrats, and 5 western white-throated woodrats.

Northern grasshopper mouse (*Onychomys leucogaster*) – The northern grasshopper mouse is generally found in arid grasslands, and our captures in the Wupatki area reflect this. We captured this species in the west half of the monument from grassland south of the entrance road, the north side of East Mesa, and the prairie dog colony just west of the Lomaki Road. There are also museum specimen records from the area of Wupatki Pueblo and Heiser Spring.

Brush mouse (*Peromyscus boylii*) – The brush mouse was the most abundant *Peromyscus* species that we captured during our sampling at Wupatki. We found this species across most of the monument, from the west boundary fence area to the Wukoki Road, and from Lomaki to Heiser Spring and Woodhouse Mesa. Most captures were in desert scrub habitat and rocky outcrops and canyon slopes. In contrast, there are very few museum specimens of brush mice from Wupatki. We found only three specimens from within the boundaries of Wupatki, and one from just south of the southern boundary. This compares to 93 specimens of deer mice and 54 specimens of pinyon mice collected in or near Wupatki. Approximately half of our trapping was at randomly-selected sites, so our results should be a good indication of relative abundance of these species, at least during the years of our sampling. We do not know whether the difference between our sampling and previous collections reflects sampling bias among the museum collections, differences in year-to-year abundance (e.g. in response to differences in rainfall), long-term changes in habitat, or some combination of these factors.

Canyon mouse (*Peromyscus crinitus*) – The canyon mouse is comparatively uncommon and local at Wupatki. True to the species' name, most of the individuals that we captured were in canyons, washes, and similar rocky areas, and most of these were in the low southeastern part of the monument. The few museum specimens, similarly, are from the area of Wupatki Pueblo, Antelope Wash, and the Antelope Wash road in the Wupatki Basin.

Deer mouse (*Peromyscus maniculatus*) – The deer mouse is moderately common and widespread in a variety of habitats at Wupatki. We found it from the west entrance road to the north boundary of the monument, south to Heiser Spring, in canyons, rocky slopes, desert scrub, and riparian habitat. We caught only one deer mouse from the Wupatki Basin, but there are museum specimens from the Antelope Wash Road in the Basin. This species may be more numerous in some years. Based on total number of museum specimens, it is second only to the pinyon mouse in specimens collected at Wupatki (however, including specimens collected near Wupatki, there are more specimens of deer mice than pinyon mice).

Pinyon mouse (*Peromyscus truei*) – The pinyon mouse is one of the most numerous species of *Peromyscus* at Wupatki, second in our trap captures only to the brush mouse. It is the most numerous *Peromyscus* in museum specimens from the monument. We found it across much of the western and central parts of the monument, south to Peshlaki Spring, but we did not find it in the easternmost parts of the monument. There are few or no pinyon pines within the boundaries of Wupatki, but this species is frequently found in areas with juniper at the monument. We also found it in rocky canyons and in desert scrub habitat in the west part of the Wupatki Basin, and at Peshlaki Spring.

Western harvest mouse (*Reithrodontomys megalotis*) – Western harvest mice are uncommon at Wupatki, but they are widely scattered from the southern extension of the monument to grasslands in the northwest. We trapped harvest mice in the vicinity of the monument visitor center, the old housing area, and the north side of East Mesa. Persons (2001), likewise, found them near the south boundary along the Wupatki Road, and two miles east of U.S. Highway 89 along the west entrance road. Museum specimens are all from the southern extent of the monument, from the vicinity of the monument headquarters and Heiser Spring. Museum specimens are much more numerous from just south of the monument's south boundary. Between 1968 and 1973, the Museum of Northern Arizona and Northern Arizona University researchers collected at least 67 harvest mice from an area one to two miles south of the south boundary. It is not clear whether this reflects a change in habitat in this area, or a period of temporary abundance, or what the reason is for the marked difference in abundance between our results and those of the earlier work.

### Family Erethizontidae – New world porcupines

North American porcupine (*Erethizon dorsatum*) – The porcupine is widespread at Wupatki, but seldom seen. It ranges from the largely open grasslands of the west end of the monument, to areas of juniper, to the desert scrub in Wupatki Basin. There is one museum record (MNA) from within the monument, from Heiser Spring. Porcupines at Wupatki take advantage of available crevices, caves, and other shelter in rock outcrops and among boulders. NPS Ranger Mary Blasing (pers. comm.) found a porcupine sheltering in a crevice between boulders in the Crack-in-the-Rock area in the northern part of the monument, miles from the nearest tree. Two observation card records note porcupines "wedged into a crack in sandstone outcrop" (New Heiser area, 29 July 1986) and "stuffed in a basalt crack" (30 July 1986, possibly near Wukoki. Location noted as "NW ¼, SE ¼, SE ¼, Section 22, on basalt outcrop below mesa top" but Township and Range were not recorded). Porcupines are also known to use earth crack caves for shelter at Wupatki, in areas where shelter is otherwise scarce (Persons and Drost 2001). Persons (2001) recorded one porcupine dead on the road, in desert scrub habitat at the south monument entrance (mile post 16), during his study of road mortality at Wupatki. We also recorded a road-killed porcupine, in grassland habitat between U.S. 89 and the Lomaki road.

## Order Carnivora – Carnivores

### Family Canidae – Dogs, foxes, and wolves

Coyote (*Canis latrans*) – Coyotes are common at Wupatki. They may be seen almost daily and one can expect to hear the sound of their yapping and howling at dawn and dusk, particularly in the Wupatki basin area. Coyotes are frequently seen abroad in open areas during the day and, based on numerous observation cards, they occur throughout the monument. We did not conduct any surveys specifically for larger mammals, but did record incidental sightings of coyotes in Cedar Canyon and in the short grass of North Mesa east of Lomaki, and noted numerous tracks in washes in the Wupatki Basin. There are at least two museum specimen records of coyote at Wupatki. The location of one (NAU Museum) is listed simply as "Wupatki," while the location of the second (MNA Museum) is "Wupatki Basin near Wupatki Nat'l Monument" (this latter record is from 1933, when the monument only included the area around Wupatki Pueblo).

Common gray fox (*Urocyon cinereoargenteus*) – Gray foxes are evidently uncommon at Wupatki. There are no museum records from in or near the monument, and we did not record any definite evidence of them, either as incidental sightings, or during night drives or at baited automatic camera set-ups. There are a few observation card records in NPS files that are presumably reliable. These include two different records of individual foxes along the entrance road "about ¼ mile east of Highway 89" in June 1963 and January 1964. We left out some other observations that were listed as "fox – red or grey?" [Red fox is not known from the Wupatki area (see Mikesic and LaRue 2003), but if the identification was this uncertain, the animal observed could have been a kit fox, as well]. Hoffmeister (1986) notes that gray foxes in Arizona are typically found in pinyon-juniper and lower habitats. The few records of gray foxes at Wupatki that we found are from the higher elevation mixed juniper / grassland areas in the western part of the monument. In contrast, kit fox records are from the desert scrub of the Wupatki Basin. Whether there is a real trend toward separation of the two species in this way is not known. Further observations may show otherwise.

Kit fox (*Vulpes macrotis*) – Sometimes lumped with the Great Plains-dwelling swift fox (*Vulpes velox*), but recent authorities (e.g. Baker et al. 2003) consider the kit fox and swift fox to be distinct. The kit fox is seldom seen at Wupatki, and all records are from the Wupatki Basin. There is one record at the Museum of Northern Arizona (NPS Flagstaff Area Monuments catalog # WUPA 25710) of a kit fox skull found along the road at the Black Falls Crossing of the Little Colorado River in June 1983. We recorded two sight observations of this species, with one individual seen late in the day about 50 m south of the Visitor Center, and a second individual seen along the road at night in the Wupatki Basin. We also found a road-killed individual on Forest Road 545 near the south boundary of Wupatki. There are two well-described records in NPS files for kit fox, both from August 1984: an individual seen along the park road south of the Visitor Center, near mile 14.5, and another record from between the Visitor Center and the south monument boundary, near milepost 15. The NPS museum for the Flagstaff National Monuments has an old kit fox skull from Merriam Crater.

### Family Procyonidae – Raccoons, ringtails, and coatis

Northern raccoon (*Procyon lotor*) – This species is frequently called simply "raccoon." Northern raccoons are rare at Wupatki, perhaps only occurring as occasional wanderers. There is one museum record (MNA) of a raccoon collected from the Wupatki Pueblo area in March 1935. This was from a time when there was more surface water at springs in this area, and conditions may have been more suitable for raccoons. There are no other museum records anywhere close to Wupatki, and we did not observe this species during our surveys. However, NPS ranger Mary Blasing observed a raccoon along the Wupatki Road at the road cut along the north base of Doney Mountain in August 2007. She stopped and was able to see this individual well at close range in the headlights of her vehicle. The best potential habitat that currently exists for raccoons at Wupatki is along the eastern edge of the monument, along the Little Colorado River.

### Family Mustelidae – Weasels, otters, and badgers

American badger (*Taxidea taxus*) – The badger is present at Wupatki, but is not common. There are three museum records of badger from Wupatki, two from MNA (Coyote Spring and Heiser Spring) and one from UA ("Wupatki, 5000 ft."). The only record of badger from our surveys was a single observation of the characteristic digging of the species, near Peshlaki Spring in September 2004. An infrared remote camera photo was also recorded of a badger in this same area, during a concurrent study by the Park Service. Nineteen records on NPS observation cards from 1940 through 1984 span the entire monument, and include the U.S. Highway 89 entrance, Magnetic Mesa, Citadel Wash, Savage Well, and Black Falls. Additional records include an individual near milepost 1 at dusk, and one just below Painted Desert Vista along the Wupatki – Sunset Crater Road. (NPS Ranger Mary Blasing, pers. comm.). The relative rarity of badger at Wupatki may be due to relatively low numbers of the ground squirrels, prairie dogs, pocket gophers, and other burrowing mammals that are its typical prey.

### Family Mephitidae – Skunks

Western spotted skunk (*Spilogale gracilis*) – Taxonomists have gone back and forth between recognizing one, wide-ranging 'spotted skunk' (*S. putorius*) in North America, and splitting this group up. Several lines of evidence point to there being more than one distinct form, and most references now consider *S. gracilis* to be a different species from the eastern spotted skunk, *S. putorius*. We list the western spotted skunk as probably present at Wupatki, but rare, based on a museum specimen (NAU) from 1 mi south of the south entrance of the monument, on the Wupatki-Sunset Crater Road (Forest Road 545). We did not observe this species during our surveys, and know of no other records in or around the monument.

### Family Felidae -- Cats

Bobcat (*Lynx rufus*) – Called *Felis rufus* by older references. Bobcats are fairly common at Wupatki. Most records are from the Wupatki Basin and adjacent canyons, but there are also records from the western part of the monument. We recorded one or more individuals using old storage buildings near Heiser Spring as daytime retreats, and we also noted sign in Deadman Wash. An adult and young were observed and photographed by NPS staff in Deadman Wash east of the main park road in 2006. There are 29 entries on NPS observation cards from 1940 – 1986, with locations including Antelope Wash, Citadel, Doney Mountain, Heiser Spring, Lomaki, and West Mesa.

Mountain lion (*Puma concolor*) – Older sources use the scientific name *Felis concolor*. There are many different common names for this wide-ranging species; the most common alternative names in our area include cougar and puma. Mountain lions probably occur in Wupatki on just an occasional basis, as wandering individuals from nearby mountain areas. During the period of our survey, radiocollared individuals ranged within a few miles of the south boundary of Wupatki, from the direction of Sunset Crater (J. Hart, USGS, pers. comm.). NPS Ranger Bill Hudson also sighted a mountain lion in Deadman Wash, which probably provides a natural travel corridor from higher elevations. In over 40 years of observation card records maintained by the National Park Service, there are only three other reports of mountain lions from within or near Wupatki. These reports vary in amount of detail provided, and reliability:

25 February 1982 – "Several tracks of an adult were seen in the soil near Old Heiser Spring. – Sheldon Smith;"

29 October 1983, 5:00 pm – "Heard ruckus of several coyotes barking and another animal responding. Mtn. lion was atop basalt flow, coyotes below on cinder slope. Mtn lion ran from one outcrop to another giving excellent silhouette. Coyotes finally disappeared over a ridge. We observed the lion for another ½ hour. Location: Feeder Cyn into Deadman's Wash, within 1 mile of WUPA – Ryan and Anderson;"

24 Aug. 1984 – "Wukoki Road. am. Visitor saw a 160 lb. cougar moving through low brush – Ed Gorney, visitor."

## Order Artiodactyla – Even-toed ungulates

### Family Cervidae – Deer

Elk (*Cervus canadensis*) – Also called *C. elaphus* by some references, and given the common name "Wapiti" in parts of its range. All of the elk in Arizona are descended from animals introduced from the Rocky Mountains. The native elk in Arizona ("Merriam's elk") is now extinct, and was not known to occur anywhere near Wupatki. Hence, we list elk at Wupatki as "non-native." Elk at Wupatki are currently uncommon or rare visitors to Wupatki. NPS Wupatki District Ranger Mary Blasing notes that in her seven years at the monument, she has seen elk just once, near milepost 8, west of Doney Mountain (a group of five females). She has recorded tracks and scat on two or three other occasions, most recently near Citadel in January 2008. Elk or their sign are most likely to be seen in the upland areas west of the Doney Cliffs, when herds move down from the nearby mountains in the fall and winter.

Mule deer (*Odocoileus hemionus*) – Mule deer are common at Wupatki, with most records from the Wupatki Basin and adjacent canyons. We did not survey specifically for large ungulates, and we did not observe mule deer during road surveys at night, nor incidentally during the course of other surveys. Observation card records of mule deer note sightings at Deadman Wash, Doney Mountain, Heiser Spring, along the Little Colorado River, in the Visitor Center area, Woodhouse Mesa, and Wukoki.

### Family Antilocapridae – Pronghorn

Pronghorn (*Antilocapra americana*) – Pronghorn are seasonally common within Wupatki, with herds sometimes numbering into the low 20's. . They are most often found in the grasslands west of the Doney Cliffs, out to U.S. Highway 89, but they occasionally venture down into the Wupatki Basin. Fence modifications on the north and south sides of the monument allow pronghorn to move in and out of these areas, onto ranch lands to the north and U.S. Forest Service lands on the south. The Highway 89 corridor appears to be essentially impermeable, however, with no crossings observed from the monument to the west side of the highway (van Riper and Ockenfels 1998). Pronghorn are occasionally killed on the road within the monument, and on Highway 89 (van Riper and Ockenfels 1998).

### Family Bovidae – Cattle, Antelope, Sheep, and Goats

Domestic cattle (*Bos taurus*) – As of 2007, domestic cattle continue to be occasional trespass visitors to Wupatki. Single individuals or small groups (three or four animals) come onto the monument from ranchlands to the south or from Navajo lands to the east, through areas where the monument fence is broken (particularly when broken sections remain open for extended periods). Recent occurrences of trespass cattle have mostly been in the Wupatki Basin, from the area of south entrance road, the north side of Deadman Wash near milepost 12, and the Crack-in-the-Rock area.

Domestic sheep (*Ovis aries*) – Also known as European Mouflon Sheep. Small numbers of domestic sheep are allowed to graze in the Wupatki Basin, under a permit to the Peshlaki family. As of 2007, numbers of these sheep are low (less than 10), and are confined to the Wupatki Basin area.

Goat (*Capra hircus*) – In addition to sheep, a few goats are kept by the Peshlaki family within the monument. There were approximately six goats within the monument in 2006 / 2007. As with the sheep, goats are evidently confined to the Wupatki Basin.

## Other potential species at Wupatki

Long-eared myotis (*Myotis evotis*) – Lincoln (1961) suggested that long-eared myotis could possibly occur at Wupatki. Chung-MacCoubrey (2005) found long-eared myotis to be common and widespread in pinyon-juniper habitat in west-central New Mexico, but at higher elevations than at Wupatki (2133 to 2573 m). The long-eared myotis may be present in low numbers, or it may occur on an occasional basis at Wupatki, but there is no evidence to confirm this.

Long-legged myotis (*Myotis volans*) – Lincoln (1961) suggested possible occurrence at WUPA. Chung-MacCoubrey (2005) found this species to be relatively numerous and widespread in pinyon-juniper habitat (at higher elevations than occur at Wupatki) in west-central New Mexico. There are no historic or recent records of long-legged myotis at or near Wupatki, but they may show up there on an occasional basis.

Western red bat (*Lasiurus blossevillii*) – In older references, the eastern and western red bats are treated as a single species (the red bat, *L. borealis*). The two species are now recognized as distinct (though nearly indistinguishable morphologically), with only the western red bat likely to be found in Arizona. Western red bats were expected by Lincoln (1961) at Wupatki, but only in migration. Records of western red bat in Arizona are few and widely scattered, with the nearest record to Wupatki being Bright Angel Creek in Grand Canyon (Hoffmeister 1986).

Mexican woodrat (*Neotoma mexicana*) – The Mexican woodrat probably reaches the lower end of its habitat range in the vicinity of Wupatki. There are two museum specimen records (Museum of Northern Arizona) of this species from about 5 km (3 miles) south of the Wupatki NM visitor center, which is approximately 1.6 km (1 mile) south of the south boundary of the monument (the two listings in the NPS Flagstaff Area Monuments database for Wupatki are assumed to be these specimens, collected outside the monument boundaries). Mexican woodrats are typically associated with coniferous forest, above the pinyon – juniper community (Hoffmeister 1986), so they are probably marginal at Wupatki, if they occur there at all.

American black bear (*Ursus americanus*) – Black bears may occur as occasional wanderers onto the monument from higher elevations – particularly following corridors such as Deadman Wash. There are no observations to suggest that bears are regular residents of the monument, however.

Ringtail (*Bassariscus astutus*) – Ringtails have not been confirmed at Wupatki. There are no definite museum or observation records from in or near Wupatki, but some of the rocky canyons and rocky escarpments within the monument may provide suitable habitat. There is an observation card in NPS files labeled "Wupatki National Monument," that lists three records of "ringtail cat (*Bassariscus astutus*)." The first record provides a good description of a ringtail, but unfortunately provides no information on specific location:

> 6 June 1979 – "Small animal, about the size of a domestic house cat. Long, bushy tail marked with black rings, entire length, 10:30 pm, J. Goldstein."

The other two records on the card clearly refer to Sunset Crater ("Base of Sunset Crater," "...end of bridge by Sunset Crater"). As noted previously, the NPS natural history observation cards for this area frequently lumped observations for both Sunset Crater and Wupatki, under "Wupatki." Long-time Wupatki District Ranger Mary Blasing notes that she has never seen this species at Wupatki, in spite of much time spent patrolling the roads at night. Similarly, Persons (2001) did not record ringtails, alive or dead, during his extensive road surveys at Wupatki.

Long-tailed weasel (*Mustela frenata*) – May occur as a rare visitor to Wupatki. Weasels have not been positively documented within the boundaries of the monument, but an individual was observed and photographed in volcanic talus east of Wupatki near Merriam Crater, at 5500 feet. The habitat where this weasel was seen is similar to areas of the eastern part of Wupatki National Monument.

Striped skunk (*Mephitis mephitis*) – Unconfirmed. Striped skunk has appeared on checklists for Wupatki NM, but we find no reliable documentation of its presence there. Lincoln (1961) reported a specimen from 8 mi N of Wupatki. This may be another species for which the combining of observations from the entire Wupatki / Sunset Crater area may have led to its erroneous listing for Wupatki, when in fact it has only been recorded at higher elevations in and around Sunset Crater.

## Species listed in error

Vagrant shrew (*Sorex vagrans*) –This record is based on a specimen at the Museum of Northern Arizona. When we examined this specimen we found it was actually a Desert Shrew, *Notiosorex crawfordi*. *Sorex vagrans* as presently understood occurs no closer to Arizona than west-central Utah and central Nevada.

Abert's squirrel (*Sciurus aberti*) – Also called tassel-eared squirrel. This species is listed on NPS observation cards from "Wupatki," without any more specific location. This record dates from a time when the Park Service managed Wupatki and Sunset Crater together. Information from many observation cards also lumps the units together, with observations being from Wupatki and/or Sunset Crater. There are no museum or observation records of Abert's squirrel any closer to Wupatki than Sunset Crater and the ponderosa pine forests of the adjacent National Forest lands. This species is closely tied to ponderosa pine, and the habitats at Wupatki are completely unsuitable for it.

# Appendix 5

## Annotated mammal species list for Sunset Crater National Monument, Arizona.

Information provided for each species includes presence or absence within the Monument, documentation (e.g. museum specimens, trap capture, or sightings), and what is known of the species' distribution and abundance. Museum abbreviations include: MNA – Museum of Northern Arizona; NAU – Northern Arizona University Vertebrate Museum; UI – University of Illinois Museum; and USNM – United States National Museum.

## Order Insectivora – Insectivores

### Family Soricidae – Shrews

Crawford's desert shrew (*Notiosorex crawfordi*) – This species is also called simply 'desert shrew' (e.g. Hoffmeister 1986). Crawford's desert shrew is evidently at least a rare resident in and around Sunset Crater National Monument. There is a museum specimen (NAU) from 1.6 km (1 mile) north of Sunset Crater. Assuming that the location description refers to Sunset Crater itself, this would put the collection location at or near the north boundary of the monument. In spite of its name, Crawford's desert shrew occurs in a wide range of habitats, from desert scrub up in elevation to areas of ponderosa pine (Armstrong and Jones 1972). The occurrence of this shrew at Sunset Crater is near the upper end of the reported elevational range for the species (Armstrong and Jones 1972).

## Order Chiroptera – Bats

### Family Vespertilionidae – Vesper Bats

Pallid bat (*Antrozous pallidus*) – We recorded calls of two separate pallid bats at Sunset Crater NM in Anabat surveys along the main road through the monument, on 9 May 2000. These represent the first records of this species in the Sunset Crater area. Of the records for pallid bat listed in Hoffmeister (1986), only two (both on the north rim of Grand Canyon) are higher than Sunset Crater, so these locations may be near the elevational limit for this species.

Big brown bat (*Eptesicus fuscus*) – We recorded a total of 14 big brown bats at Sunset Crater NM during Anabat surveys, the highest numbers of any bat that we recorded in this area. There is also a museum specimen (MNA) from Medicine Valley, about 3.2 km (2 miles) west of the Sunset Crater west boundary.

Hoary bat (*Lasiurus cinereus*) – One of the most fortuitous records in our Anabat surveys at Sunset Crater NM was our recording of a hoary bat on 9 May 2000 – the first record of this species from Sunset Crater and the surrounding area. In this region, hoary bats appear to be primarily migratory, passing through on their spring and fall transits of northern Arizona. One of our spring surveys was during the migration 'window' of the species, and the individual that we recorded may have been passing through the monument during its northward travels. There are relatively few records of hoary bat in northern Arizona (Hoffmeister 1986, and records at MNA). We do not know whether this is a true reflection of their relative rarity, or simply a result of the difficulty of detecting them (or perhaps a combination of the two factors).

California myotis (*Myotis californicus*) – We encountered one or two California myotis in our Anabat surveys at Sunset Crater. The first record was in a survey along the main road on 9 May 2000. The second record was also during a driving survey along the main road, on 14 October 2000. This recording was not as clear, but was in the right frequency range for California myotis and was thought to be that species. This span of time – mid-spring to mid fall – probably pretty well brackets the activity period of the species at this elevation.

Western small-footed myotis (*Myotis ciliolabrum*) – This species is sometimes treated under the name *M. leibii* (e.g. Hoffmeister 1986) and also *M. subulatus* (e.g. Burt and Grossenheider 1976). Formerly, it was thought that there was one 'small-footed myotis' that occurred across North America. It is now recognized that there are two species – an eastern form (*M. leibii*) and a western form (*M. ciliolabrum*). We recorded only a single western small-footed myotis at Sunset Crater. There is also a museum specimen (MNA) from Medicine Valley, about 3.2 km (2 miles) west of Sunset Crater, 2160 m (7100 ft.) elevation. This is a higher elevation species and it is probably fairly common at Sunset Crater, in spite of the few records.

Long-eared myotis (*Myotis evotis*) – Though we only recorded a single long-eared myotis at Sunset Crater, in an Anabat survey on 9 May 2000, we expect this species is fairly common in and around Sunset Crater NM. The long-eared myotis is a typical species of the ponderosa pine woodlands in the Flagstaff area. Chung-MacCoubrey (2005) found them to be common and widespread in pinyon-juniper habitat in west-central New Mexico, at comparable elevations to Sunset Crater (2133 to 2573 m), so they are most likely a regular breeding resident of the monument.

Fringed myotis (*Myotis thysanodes*) – We recorded at least two fringed myotis in Anabat surveys at Sunset Crater NM, in the spring (early May) and fall (mid-October). Our recording of this species is the first record for the Sunset Crater area, though they are fairly common at the lower elevations of Wupatki (this study). Fringed myotis occurs in habitats ranging from chaparral and oak woodland, into ponderosa pine forest (Hoffmeister 1986), so occurrence of the species at Sunset Crater is not surprising. At Wupatki this species uses basalt earth cracks as roost sites, and they may use similar sites lava caves at Sunset Crater.

Long-legged myotis (*Myotis volans*) – We recorded a single long-legged myotis at Sunset Crater NM during an Anabat survey on 9 May 2000. This is the first record of the species within Sunset Crater NM. Chung-MacCoubrey (2005) found these bats to be relatively numerous and widespread in pinyon-juniper habitat in west-central New Mexico, at similar elevations to Sunset Crater. The long-legged myotis will probably be found to be a fairly common breeding resident at Sunset Crater.

Western pipistrelle (*Pipistrellus hesperus*) – We recorded a single western pipistrelle during spring Anabat surveys at Sunset Crater NM. Pipistrelles in Arizona cover a wide elevational range, from low-elevation creosote bush desert to spruce-fir forests, usually near cliffs and canyon areas (Hoffmeister 1986). This is typically an early-flying species, frequently abroad in the late afternoon or early evening, while the sky is still quite light.

### Family Molossidae – Free-tailed bats

Brazilian free-tailed bat (*Tadarida brasiliensis*) – Many references use the common name "Mexican free-tailed bat" for this species. A lone Brazilian free-tailed bat was recorded during Anabat surveys at Sunset Crater NM, on 9 May 2000. This species roosts in medium-sized to very large colonies numbering millions of individuals. They may travel long distances from their roosts (up to 30 km or more), so the individual that we recorded at Sunset Crater may have come from a roost some distance away. We do not know of any roosts within Sunset Crater NM.

## Order Lagomorpha – Pikas, hares, and rabbits

### Family Leporidae – Hares and rabbits

Black-tailed jackrabbit (*Lepus californicus*) – Black-tailed jackrabbits are present at Sunset Crater NM, but seem to be relatively uncommon based on the few observation records. The NPS Flagstaff-area National Monuments museum has 16 natural history observation cards for this species, over the period 1950–1969.

Desert cottontail (*Sylvilagus audubonii*) – Desert cottontails occur at Sunset Crater, but appear to be relatively uncommon. They are only occasionally seen along or crossing the road at night. One museum specimen (MNA) was collected "1 mi E of Sunset Crater." Cottontails are more numerous in grassy areas outside of the monument boundary, such as Bonito Park. They are numerous in the grasslands at Wupatki.

## Order Rodentia – Rodents

### Family Sciuridae – Squirrels

White-tailed antelope squirrel (*Ammospermophilus leucurus*) – The occurrence of this species at Sunset Crater NM is based on a single museum specimen (UI), from the "NE edge Sunset Crater Natl. Mon." (Hoffmeister 1986). There are no NPS observation cards that we could find for this species at Sunset Crater. Hoffmeister (1986) notes that this species reaches the upper end of its habitat range in the "lower part of the juniper belt," so it is not surprising that it is rare at Sunset Crater.

Gray-collared chipmunk (*Neotamias cinereicollis*) – Called *Tamias cinereicollis* or *Eutamias cinereicollis* by other sources. There are three specimens of gray-collared chipmunk from the area of Jack Smith Tank, about 3 km (2 miles) west of the west boundary of Sunset Crater National Monument. We did not conduct diurnal small mammal surveys at Sunset Crater, and NPS observation card records for Sunset Crater simply refer to "chipmunks." The gray-collared chipmunk occurs in ponderosa pine and spruce-fir forest throughout this region, though, and is presumed to be fairly common at Sunset Crater. The gray-collared chipmunk has bold light and dark stripes on its back, easily distinguishing it from the cliff chipmunk (the only other species in the area), which is dark gray on the back, with indistinct stripes.

Cliff chipmunk (*Neotamias dorsalis*) – This species is called *Tamias dorsalis* or *Eutamias dorsalis* by other sources (e.g. Hoffmeister 1986, Reid 2006). There are probably two chipmunk species that occur at Sunset Crater National Monument. The cliff chipmunk is known from the monument from a museum specimen (MNA) killed on the road in March 1972. Two additional museum specimens (also MNA) were collected 8 km (5 miles) east of Sunset Crater. The cliff chipmunk is a rock chipmunk that is frequently found at lower elevations, though it does range up into ponderosa pine forest. The dark gray coloration that covers the back of this species largely obscures the light stripes – making it very easy to distinguish from the boldly-striped gray-collared chipmunk, which also occurs in the Sunset Crater area.

Abert's squirrel (*Sciurus aberti*) – Abert's squirrel is a common species at Sunset Crater. Some of the natural history observation card records in the museum files of the NPS Flagstaff-area National Monuments note "seen daily," "several," "as many as 10 along road," "12-15." Several additional cards noted individuals killed along the main road through the monument. Observations recorded on record cards span at least May through November. The NAU Vertebrate Museum has two specimens of Abert's squirrel collected from Sunset Crater NM. The Museum of Northern Arizona has three specimens collected nearby, from Medicine Valley (about 3 km west of Sunset Crater NM), from "Bonito Flat," and from "E of Sunset Crater Nat'l Mon. boundary 3 mi. on FS Rd 545." There is also an MNA specimen (listed in the NPS Flagstaff Area National Monuments database as catalog # WUPA 10613) from the Cinder Hills area. This specimen has previously been included with mammal specimens from Wupatki (perhaps because of the past practice of lumping records from Wupatki and Sunset Crater, as noted previously), and may be the reason for the erroneous listing of Abert's squirrels as occurring at Wupatki.

Golden-mantled ground squirrel (*Spermophilus lateralis*) – There is one museum specimen (MNA) of golden-mantled ground squirrel that was collected from "Medicine Valley, San Francisco Mtns." This is about 3 km (2 miles) west of the west boundary of Sunset Crater. Surprisingly, this is the only record we could find of this species near Sunset Crater. This is a common species of coniferous forests in the Flagstaff area, occasionally ranging down into pinyon-juniper (Hoffmeister 1986). It is also one of the species that frequently becomes semi-tame around campgrounds and visitor areas. We suspect this species occurs at Sunset Crater, but the lack of records is puzzling.

Rock squirrel (*Spermophilus variegatus*) – An old scientific name is *Citellus variegatus*. Rock squirrels are common resident over much of Sunset Crater NM. There are four museum specimens from in or near the monument. Two of these (NAU) are from "Sunset Crater," and two (MNA) are from Jack Smith Tank, about 3 km (2 mi.) west of the Sunset Crater NM west boundary. Observation card records range from April through September, with the species noted as "numerous" at times in mid- to late summer. Some cards specifically note rock squirrels around the lava flow area and visitor parking area, with occasional individuals killed on the road.

## Family Geomyidae – Pocket gophers

Botta's pocket gopher (*Thomomys bottae*) – Botta's pocket gopher appears to be at least a rare resident at Sunset Crater NM, but no surveys have been conducted specifically for these burrowing mammals. An observation card record from 19 September 1968 noted an individual that was found "running around in middle of road" at 9 pm, near the Cinder Hills overlook. The card notes that the individual was "identified and released." There are two museum records (both UI) from near the southwest boundary of the monument: "2 mi SW Sunset Crater Nat. Mon." and "10 mi NE Flagstaff, 4 mi SW Sunset Crater NM."

## Family Muridae – Mice, rats, and voles

Mexican woodrat (*Neotoma mexicana*) – Mexican woodrats are present at Sunset Crater, where they are probably fairly common residents. There are two museum specimens from within the boundaries of Sunset Crater (both from Bonito Lava Flow; NAU) and two additional specimens (MNA) from Jack Smith Tank, about 3 km (2 mi.) west of Sunset Crater west boundary.

Stephens's woodrat (*Neotoma stephensi*) – Stephens's woodrat is almost certainly present in at least small numbers at Sunset Crater. Two museum specimens (NAU) from 8 km (5 mi) east and about 10 km (6 mi) northeast of Sunset Crater are the closest documented records that we found to the monument. However, this species is common in pinyon-juniper habitats, and also ranges up into ponderosa pine woodlands (Hoffmeister 1986). The lack of records from Sunset Crater presumably just reflects the lack of targeted survey effort in and near the monument.

Northern grasshopper mouse (*Onychomys leucogaster*) – The northern grasshopper mouse is most likely present at Sunset Crater, though it is probably not common. A museum specimen (USNM) from "Cedar belt east of O'Leary Peak" is about 1.5 km (1 mi.) north of the Sunset Crater NM boundary.

Brush mouse (*Peromyscus boylii*) – Brush mice are probably fairly common at Sunset Crater. The nearest museum specimen (NAU) that we found is from "Flagstaff, park near Sunset"—presumably referring to Bonito Park. The NAU museum has four additional specimens of brush mice from "5 miles E of Sunset Crater" (about 8 km). Brush mice occur in a wide range of habitats in Arizona, including at elevations as high or higher than Sunset Crater. Future trapping at Sunset Crater NM should document this species there.

Deer mouse (*Peromyscus maniculatus*) – Based on museum specimens, this is the most frequently captured *Peromyscus* species in the Sunset Crater area. The Museum of Northern Arizona, the NAU Vertebrate Museum, and the University of Illinois Museum have three specimens from within the boundaries of Sunset Crater and 14 more from the surrounding area (Jack Smith Tank, Medicine Valley, and "5 miles east of Sunset Crater." One of the MNA specimens is from "South rim of Sunset Crater," so deer mice reach the highest elevations within the monument.

Pinyon mouse (*Peromyscus truei*) – The pinyon mouse is probably fairly common at Sunset Crater NM. Of 10 museum specimens (3 MNA, 6 NAU, 1 UI) collected in the vicinity of the monument, 2 were judged to be within the boundaries: one specimen "0.5 mi E of Sunset Crater" (MNA); and one at "NE edge Sunset Crater National Mon." (UI). Pinyon mice are most numerous in pinyon pine woodlands or pinyon-juniper associations, but do range into higher and lower elevation habitats.

Western harvest mouse (*Reithrodontomys megalotis*) – Though we do not know of any specimens or observations from directly within the boundaries of Sunset Crater NM, this species is probably present in suitable dense, grassy habitats at the monument. The Northern Arizona University Vertebrate Museum has a harvest mouse specimen that was collected "13 miles NNE of Flagstaff," and the University of Illinois Museum has two specimens, one from "10 miles NE Flagstaff, 4 miles SW Sunset Crater NM" and the other from "2 miles SW Sunset Crater Nat. Mon." Areas of Bonito Park probably provide particularly good habitat for harvest mice.

### Family Erethizontidae – New World porcupines

North American porcupine (*Erethizon dorsatum*) – Porcupines are present at Sunset Crater, but there are relatively few observation card records. Several of the observations are of individuals on or along the road in Bonito Park or near the campground. An adult and young porcupine "were observed crossing road about ½ mile west of the campground" on June 28, 1971. Other records include: milepost 32 along FR 545 (22 May 1988); and "immature crawling along roadside ½ mi. east of contact station at dusk….eventually crawled down slope and then climbed into a ponderosa pine (October 1971). There is one museum specimen (Museum of Vertebrate Zoology, University of California, Berkeley) collected on O'Leary Peak.

## Order Carnivora – Carnivores

### Family Canidae – Dogs, foxes, and wolves

Coyote (*Canis latrans*) – Coyotes are fairly common in and around Sunset Crater, where they are often seen crossing the road or hunting in Bonito Park. They are occasionally found killed on the road. Observation cards have noted pups out of the den from late June through early August. Other observations include: "…pair hunting on rim of Lenox Crater at 1900" (11 May 1964); pup on road – 9" – 10" tall, Sunset Crater nature trail area (8 August 1988); 2 adults, 1 pup, Painted Desert (11 August 1988); Sunset Crater west boundary – young of year, dead on road (10 October 1986).

Common gray fox (*Urocyon cinereoargenteus*) – Judging from observation cards, the gray fox appears to be an uncommon (or at least infrequently seen) resident of Sunset Crater NM. Most observations are of individuals along or crossing the main road at night, including: "…on the Loop Road at a distance of about ½ mile east of the Sunset Crater N.M. boundary. Time – 10 pm" (13 March 1959); and at edge of lava flow opposite west Sunset Crater entrance sign, 5 pm (24 June 1988). There are twelve observation card records from 1960 – 1974, most of them during the summer months (June through September).

### Family Ursidae – Bears

American black bear (*Ursus americanus*) – Black bears appear to rare residents or occasional visitors to the Sunset Crater area. An observation card from 19 July 1965 notes "one reported by visitors (1125) crossing road N of crater, running westward along canyon & turning straight up the crater. Track measured 7" from heel to foremost claws." Another dated 6 June 1988 records a "medium brown" individual that came down a cinder slope and crossed the monument road near milepost 30 at about 5:10 pm. A third card noted tracks only: "Tracks of one bear were observed where it had travelled ¼ mile along cinder road near dump" (19 June 1964).

### Family Procyonidae – Raccoons, ringtails, and coatis

Ringtail (*Bassariscus astutus*) – Also called "ringtail cat," this small, slender, long-tailed relative of the raccoon is present at Sunset Crater NM, and is probably fairly common. Ringtails are rarely seen but are frequently overlooked due to their strictly nocturnal habits and generally shy behavior. Of 20 observation record cards reviewed (most from 1960 – 1988), most reports were of individuals seen crossing the monument road, or seen around the visitor contact station or housing area in the late evening. Some reports note individuals up in, or climbing, trees, including ponderosa pines. One card notes a ringtail "…at end of bridge by Sunset Crater, ran across road then up a ponderosa pine by road. Climbed to top of tree" (11 July 1986). There is one observation of a ringtail retreating into a lava crack in the lava flow area (18 October 1970). An individual away from the visitor center and housing area was along FR 545 on the north side of Lenox Crater, on 3 September 1988 at 8:30 pm. The most recent report of a ringtail is an individual observed in the Lava Flow Parking Area in December 2007 at approximately 2100 hours, by NPS Ranger Mary Blasing. There are no museum records from near Sunset Crater, but there is a record card of a road-killed ringtail on U.S. Highway 89 near the Sunset Crater entrance road.

Northern raccoon (*Procyon lotor*) – Northern raccoons are present at least in small numbers at Sunset Crater NM. They are known from the vicinity of the campground and Visitor Center / developed area, but we have not found any records at Sunset Crater away from this. During the course of our surveys, we saw small groups of 3 – 4 raccoons (presumed to be family groups) along the road in the campground area. We did not find any observation cards for this familiar species in the NPS Flagstaff Area Monuments files, and wonder if this indicates that raccoons have only recently taken up residence in the area. Raccoons at Sunset Crater may be dependent on developed areas for water and possibly enhanced foraging opportunities.

### Family Mustelidae – Weasels, Otters, and Badgers

Long-tailed weasel (*Mustela frenata*) – Long-tailed weasels are evidently uncommon residents at Sunset Crater, with relatively few sightings recorded. There is one museum specimen (road kill, MNA) from Bonito Park, just west of the Sunset Crater NM boundary, that was picked up on 17 July 1972. An interesting observation record from 23 June 1966, 0910 hours, reads: "One chased a chipmunk up a tree just west of the contact station (about 100 feet) and then disappeared down a hole in the lava bed." Other records include: FR 545 ¼ mi E US 89, 10 pm (9 August 1988); one ran across road near Bonito Lava Flow pullout (5 November 1965); and one "in white winter coat" in hole along shoulder of road through Bonito Park (23 November 1971).

American badger (*Taxidea taxus)* – Badgers are present at Sunset Crater, but they are not common. One natural history observation card notes an individual "taking a drink from the bird bath in front of the new quarters at the Visitor Center" on 28 November 1968. Another card notes that a "family of badgers have been living in a den near the "life zones" exhibit during the summer" (September 1964). The nearest museum record (USNM) to Sunset Crater is from "Black Bill Park, 12 mi NE of Flagstaff."

### Family Mephitidae – Skunks

<u>Striped skunk</u> (*Mephitis mephitis*) – Striped skunks appear to be relatively rare in the Sunset Crater area. There are no museum specimens for the area, and we did not record any during night surveys. Most observations of striped skunks have been on the roads or around the Bonito campground and housing area. Of 18 individual striped skunks recorded on observation cards between 1963 and 1988, the majority (11) were seen on or crossing the roads. A family group of five striped skunks was noted on August 20, 1965 near the west boundary of the monument. Other observations include: "…two, about 8:30 pm, in a light snow storm on the road through Bonita Park…" (3 March 1969); "one skunk in Bonito CG 'hassling campers'" (29 July 1974); Bonito campground amphitheater, 8:30 pm (10 June 1988); Bonito campground amphitheater (9 July 1988); and "fr 545 at base of sunset crater, 10:15 pm" (9 august 1988).

<u>Western spotted skunk</u> (*Spilogale gracilis*) – Probable resident or visitor to Sunset Crater National Monument. A road-killed specimen was found but not collected in June 1985 approximately 2.4 km (1.5 mi.) east of the Sunset Crater east boundary, along FR 545 ("2 miles SW Painted Desert Vista, USFS 545" – S. Cinnamon, NPS Observation Card).

### Family Felidae – Cats

<u>Bobcat</u> (*Lynx rufus*) – Older references use the scientific name *Felis rufus*. Bobcats are present at Sunset Crater NM, but there are few observation record cards for them. These include: "1 large bobcat on several occasions in cinder fields south of crater in early mornings…" (May 1964); and "One was observed in the process of stalking an Abert squirrel early this morning near … base of Lennox Crater" (11 May 1964); "Bobcat tracks observed near dump" (November 1964); and "one observed N of road at 'Life Zones' exhibit" (17 July 1965).

<u>Mountain lion</u> (*Puma concolor*) – Also called 'cougar' or 'puma,' among other common names; older references give the scientific name as *Felis concolor*. Mountain lions are occasional visitors or uncommon residents at Sunset Crater, but are seldom seen. In an ongoing study of distribution, habitat, and prey habits of mountain lions in the Flagstaff area, radiocollared lions have been recorded in and around Sunset Crater on a regular basis (J. Hart, USGS Southwest Biological Science Center, pers. comm. 2007). Mountain lions are primarily crepuscular or nocturnal and are wary in their habits, so they are rarely seen: over a 60-year span (1940's through the present), there are 11 observation card records of lions, most of them noting tracks or individuals crossing the road. Some of these include: "Single large adult observed along loop road just north of Sunset Crater…" (October 1956); "Tracks observed crossing entrance road near Lenox Crater in the snow: (1 November 1956); "One observed crossing road at Bonita Park at 2115 hours…" (24 August 1967); "Walked across 545 ¼ mi from E SUCR boundary" (28 July 1988, Range 8 E, Township 23 N, Section 22, NE 1/4); "Ran across road just W of Lava Flow pullout, 10:10 pm" (22 September 1988); and "Single adult was seen east of highway travelling north, saw vehicle and went downhill to the east. N of Painted Desert Vista, 1430 hrs., H. John" (December 1981).

## Order Artiodactyla – Even-toed ungulates

### Family Cervidae – Deer

<u>Elk</u> (*Cervus canadensis*) – Called *C. elaphus* in many references, and given the common name "Wapiti" in parts of its range. Fairly common in and around Sunset Crater; recorded in most months of the year. Observation card information suggests that elk may have increased in abundance over recent decades. Many observations are in Bonito Park, e.g. 30 May 1988, 11 January 1989. Other records include: "two E of residence area, 7:30 pm" (30 June 1988); "15-20 along FR 545B near Sunset" (31 July 1989); "FR 545 near MP 35, 7:50 pm" (4 August 1988); four at MP 34 – "ran across road" (2 September 1988); "elk tracks on road behind housing area, towards Bonito Park" (31 December 1988).

<u>Mule deer</u> (*Odocoileus hemionus*) – Mule deer are fairly common residents at Sunset Crater, and occur through most or all of the year. Some specific observations throughout the year include: buck + 10 does 2 mi. N of Desert View (21 February 1989); nine, west of Bonito Park pullout, 4 pm (22 February 1988); five at FR 244 & FR 545 (16 March 1986); one at MP 30.2, walking up Sunset Crater (22 July 1988); 13, one mi. E of US 89, SUCR (3 August 1988); doe + 2 fawns, SW exposure of Sunset Crater (22 August 1982); FR 545, app. MP 35 (26 August 1988); one male at MP 34, Sunset Crater (29 August 1988); 11 south of Bonito Park (1 September 1988); one at MP 34, FR 545 (21 September 1988); 10 at FR 545 & FR 414 (16 October 1988); between FR 414 and housing (20 & 21 October 1988); six at MP 30, west side Sunset Crater (22 October 1986); 16 at Bonito Park (22 October 1986); three at Bonito Park (24 October 1988); seven

at Bonito Park (28 October 1988);  NW face Sunset Crater (5 November 1984);  one female, FR 545 and FR 414 (9 November 1988).

### Family Antilocapridae – Pronghorn

Pronghorn (*Antilocapra americana*) –Pronghorn are frequently observed in Bonito Park, and are also seen along the Sunset Crater – Wupatki Road. They are presumably occasional transients within the boundaries of Sunset Crater NM. Some specific observation records (from NPS natural history observation cards) include: 7, 21, & 29 June 1983 – 4 to 5 each day in Bonito Park; July 1989 – 7-14 individuals on 4 dates during month; 16 July 1988 – 2 at Bonito Park; 19 July 1988 – 2 at Bonito Park; 8 August 1983 – 9, 1.6 km (1 mile) south of Painted Desert overlook; 6 September 1988 – two east of Painted Desert. There is one museum specimen (USNM) from "12 miles northeast of Flagstaff, 6800 ft.," which is in the approximate location of Black Bill Park, southwest of Sunset Crater NM.

### Family Bovidae – Cattle, antelope, sheep, and goats

Domestic sheep (*Ovis aries*) – Also called European Mouflon Sheep, domestic (and probably feral and semi-feral) sheep were found historically in the area around Sunset Crater, at least on an occasional or seasonal basis. Sheep were formerly grazed and herded in the lands around Flagstaff (including the area that is now Wupatki NM) and up into the San Francisco Peaks. The Museum of Northern Arizona has a specimen collected in 1954 from "Near entrance road to Sunset Nat'l Monument."

Bighorn sheep (*Ovis canadensis*) – We list bighorn sheep as "Historic" for Sunset Crater NM. They were probably former residents or at least occasional visitors to the area. A museum record (USNM) from Mt. Elden is the nearest record that we have found to Sunset Crater. The subspecies that formerly occurred in the area of Sunset Crater was the desert bighorn, (*O. canadensis mexicana* or *O. canadensis nelsoni*, depending on the author – e.g. Hoffmeister 1986, McCutchen 1995).

## Other potential species at Sunset Crater:

Merriam's shrew (*Sorex merriami*) – One museum specimen (MNA) of this species was collected on 8 December 1969 from "13 mi. NNE of Flagstaff." This is in the general area of Sunset Crater, perhaps close to Bonito Park. Hoffmeister (1986) describes habitat for this species as "cool grassy places...near coniferous forests," and Armstrong and Jones (1971) note that Merriam's shrew occurs in drier habitats than other *Sorex* species, including pine – Douglas fir – aspen woodlands. Shrews are notoriously under-represented in most mammal surveys (including our work) and it seems likely this species will be found at Sunset Crater NM in the future.

Silky pocket mouse (*Perognathus flavus*) – There are two museum specimens (UI) from 3 km (2 mi.) and 6 km (4 mi.) southwest of Sunset Crater. If these descriptions refer to Sunset Crater itself, then the first record is within 1.5 km (1 mi.) of the south boundary of the monument. Silky pocket mice range up into juniper areas (Hoffmeister 1986) and it is likely that future surveys will find them within the boundaries of Sunset Crater NM.

Ord's kangaroo rat (*Dipodomys ordii*) – There is a National Park Service record card for "Kangaroo Rat" for Sunset Crater, dated 13 July 1969. The card states: "9:30 pm  One going right down the middle of the road by the cinder hills, N.E. corner of Sunset Crater. Long tail unmistakable, easily identified. DEM" Ord's kangaroo rats are typically found in fine soils or sandy substrates, in desert shrub and grassland communities, occasionally ranging up into pinyon-juniper (Hoffmeister 1986). The habitat in and around Sunset Crater NM is decidedly uncharacteristic, and we know of no other reports of kangaroo rats close to Sunset Crater. We are doubtful of this report.

Western white-throated woodrat (*Neotoma albigula*) – Called also simply "white-throated woodrat." The nearest museum and trapping records of this species to Sunset Crater are from Wupatki, to the north, and Winona, to the south. Most or all of the records listed in Hoffmeister (1986) are lower in elevation than Sunset Crater. Hoffmeister (1986) also notes, however, that western white-throated woodrats "frequently are encountered in pinyon-juniper" so it is possible that they may be found at Sunset Crater.

## Erroneous records

<u>Short-tailed weasel</u> (*Mustela erminea*) – An observation card for this species is on file at the Flagstaff Monuments

Headquarters, dated 25 October 1974, from "Bonito Lava Flow approx. 1 mile west of crater." Although the description is of an animal seen at close range for several minutes, no details are provided on the identification. Short-tailed weasel has never been recorded from the state of Arizona, and this sighting probably refers to the long-tailed weasel.

NPS 360/100791, December 2009